Cancel Cable
How Internet Pirates Get Free Stuff

CHRIS FEHILY

Questing Vole Press

Cancel Cable: How Internet Pirates Get Free Stuff
By Chris Fehily

v 1.01

For Bo

Contents

Part IV: Torrent Categories

1 The Terrain

Free for the taking: an internet bounty of shared movies, TV shows, music, video games, fonts, books, software, photos, and anything that can be digitized and copied. What's the catch?

Lawyers

Depending on where you live and what you share, file sharing might be unlawful. Only in the United States are these laws enforced with any vigor. (Most of what's shared is produced in the US, and protecting American intellectual property isn't a concern for other nations.) Under US law, the crime is copyright infringement, a term so fatiguing that interest groups rechristened it piracy. Infringement leaves the original work intact and isn't piracy (or theft) in the common sense, but that's what happens when your opponent controls the language of the debate. The enforcement and awareness campaigns of copyright holders have been so grasping and ham-handed, however, that ordinary people now call themselves pirates, either matter-of-factly or defiantly.

My own Damascus Road came while watching a Hollywood propagandette featuring a backstage nobody griping about movie pirates picking his pockets. Considering the enormous money and influence at play put me in mind of the banker who enjoys an $800 lunch at Masa before dashing off a note to a finance minister about the austerity program.

File-sharing news at TorrentFreak (*torrentfreak.com*) reports the regular failures of copyright holders and their enforcers. They pushed through their own laws by using the usual methods but then got lazy, unwisely listening to litigators rather than public-relations consultants, who would have counseled them to:

- Censor the internet via political pressure on weak internet service providers.

- Hire a PR flack to design a campaign to convince the bewildered herd that file sharing is a threat to their entitlements.

- Apply power from the top and protect it from the bottom. Convince cops that intellectual property is *real* property. Cops, paid with property taxes, are more vigilant about property-related crimes than violent ones.

If you live in the United States, read this book as you would one about evading taxes or creating home meth labs. Elsewhere, officials enforce intellectual-property laws mincingly, prosecuting people they dislike or tossing the odd pirate to a US trading partner or domestic front group.

Victims

The US, the UK, France, and a few other late-stage mercantilists have piracy laws with nontrivial punishments. Though these laws are mostly unenforced (it's career and spiritual death for public prosecutors), private lawyers still love them.

In the US, for example, entrepreneurial lawyers buddy up with producers of low-grossing movies, threaten downloaders en masse, and then split the settlements. "Threaten" not "summon," and "settlements" not "awards." These suits aren't intended to go to court. The targets are told to pay up or be sued for serious cash. The sweet spot appears to be a $1500–$2500 settlement, an amount that most people, guilty or not, will pay to make a lawyer go away. Ensnared pirates who pay the settlement still don't do badly; after all, they've *saved* a mountain of cash over the years by not paying for stuff they've downloaded. UK lawyers run a similar racket. It's a growth industry.

As a scare tactic, US industry groups (usually the MPAA and RIAA) sometimes sue people and pirate websites in court. Court-imposed fines are huge, though these crimes should be on par with shoplifting.

Q&A

Q: The world's full of lawyers who dispense injustice. So what?

A: No real effort is made to establish guilt. The technology that fingers downloaders is flawed and casts a wide net. Corpses and network printers have been threatened.

Q: Collateral damage aside, didn't these pirates get what was coming?

A: Startup idea: License or create copyrighted material. Dangle it on pirate sites and sue Americans who bite. Profit!

Q: Won't encouraging piracy drum up business for these lawyers?

A: Most books have no measurable effect, and piracy is legal or near riskless for most of humanity.

Q: Don't artists have the right to make a living from their work?

A: It's a desire, not a right.

Q: And small businesses?

A: New sellers of knitting patterns, fonts, comic books, guitar lessons, and fashion designs learn that such things have long been shared online. To be surprised or embittered invites more schadenfreude than sympathy.

Q: And you?

A: This book is headed for pirate sites with or without my consent. Even if I sell it in only paperback format, someone will photocopy it and post it online, or someone at the printer will swipe the PDF and post it. Or, some book reviewer's kid will do it. But they won't have to because *I* am going to post it, heading off low-quality or expurgated copies. If pirates hurt sales of the for-pay versions, I'll find another way to make money. Musicians give concerts. Artists get patrons. Writers speak.

Q: I've read about people getting busted for piracy and paying huge fines — isn't file-sharing riskier than you imply?

A: You've also read about fraud busts at tax time and drug busts before elections. News is by definition the reporting of rare events. When trivial or commonplace events are treated as news, ask yourself, "Why now?" and "Who benefits?" Most drugs-in-our-schools stories, for example, are scripted in the studio. A reporter and cameraman, rather than wander the halls until Judgment looking for an actual dealer, find a kid who'll agree, "Sure, I'll say I sell drugs in school on camera." With few exceptions, laws are written to advantage their writers. Interested parties, not legislators, draft copyright laws and use the press to create the illusion of enforcement. When calculating the probability of being caught, consider in your denominator that piracy accounts for at least a quarter of worldwide internet traffic.

Q: Still, isn't piracy a bit dishonorable?

A: Honor is unimportant in my society, but my understanding is that it's something earned and not tarnished except by the shame of the acquirer. One's honor is not at the discretion of counter-pirates. Twinge of conscience? Tell yourself that you never would have bought what you're downloading for free, so the owners incur no loss. As for the goals of the creative class, fame and attractive lovers trump money.

Benefits
Here's what you're missing:

Zero cost. Everything that you download is free free free.

No shame. I've worked in and around Silicon Valley for more than 15 years, and I have yet to meet anyone privately concerned with the legality of anything downloaded over the internet.

Fillerless. TV shows have no ads. Movies have no menus, unskippable content, autoplay ads, forced user input, or copythreats.

Minimal wait. That new episode of *Doctor Who* is available for download worldwide minutes after it airs on the BBC. Unedited Olympic, World Cup, NFL, and other sports events are posted right after the final whistle (no TV time-shifting).

No DRM. Digital rights management (DRM) is broken or bypassed in pirate downloads. DRM prevents you from watching, playing, hearing, reading, opening, or copying something whenever and wherever you want. Retail DVDs, for example, are region-coded to play only in specific parts of the world. Retail music, games, ebooks, and software often have

DRM restrictions too. (DRM isn't about impeding pirates but repeatedly selling ordinary customers the same content in different formats.)

Opt out.   Every act of piracy nibbles at the world of enforcers, patent trolls, ad agencies, techno-optimists, free-marketeers, agents, graphic designers, and flag wavers.

Positive liberty.   Pirates' actions embody the system that they want to create: self-organization, mutual aid, direct action, autonomy, voluntary association, opposition to power, exposure and subversion of coercive institutions, and means consonant with ends.

Worldliness.   A pirate interprets the headline "US judge orders piracy website to remove all links to infringing content" to mean:

- The website's owner isn't a US citizen or resident.

- The claimant's lawyers burned through large fees navigating the site's corporate labyrinth.

- The owner is deciding whether to redomicile and colo the site to Gibralter, Curaçao, or the Isle of Man.

- If the site shuts down or bars Americans, alternatives abound.

- The owner is letting the judge keep his dignity by sending a lawyer and filling out forms now and then, but otherwise ignores the court.

Free marketing.   Is that book, song, or movie of yours going nowhere? Give it to pirates and maybe get some word-of-mouth. The evidence that piracy actually hurts sales is flawed and unconvincing — plenty of authors, musicians, and filmmakers freely post their works on the internet.

Enlightenment.   Pirates tend not to assign value based on cost; they look askance at people who pay for what's free, and consider copyright and patent laws to be a barbaric assault on the imagination.

Soothing.   Piracy reduces your regret at not having lived a life of crime. Taking freely from creatives tempers your resentment of people more talented, richer, and luckier than you who reject your life as blank.

About This Book

A benefit of living in a society that fears its own machines is the lucrative market for computer how-to guides. This book has the trappings of modern tutorials—limited scope, task-based steps, bulleted lists, visual aids—and some deliberate lies to make it easier for you to learn ideas and techniques. You'll find exceptions to informally introduced rules in later chapters and as you become a more-skillful pirate.

Every book expresses its author's unhappiness with existing books, which would be the case here if there were similar books to be unhappy about. I found one, but it's so preachy and wishy-washy that its authors must be near suicide for letting their publisher hamstring them. Self-censoring is no way for a writer to spend his brief flash on earth. I pitched this book to a few majors and heard "We can't touch it—we're *about* copyright" and "Forget it. Publishing it would annoy our other authors." (Publishers think that writers care about publishers and other writers.)

The idea for this book came when I attended a keynote speech by an Apple kahuna. When he announced that the company had sold x billion songs for $0.99 each, people applauded thunderously. Not just the Apple employees in their civvies, but ordinary geeks and even reporters.

Billions of songs. People still pay for recorded music? Billions. There's a book here. And not one of those crappy midlists I've been writing. Man, that guy's, what, 55? and looks like death. And not some pop Spenglerian crap about losers cheering corporations. Yikes, if I had stock in this company I'd be posting lookouts 24/7 outside Stanford Hospital. I'll need a catchy title. "Bankrupt Hollywood." No. Stupid. Besides, the studios might hire me to push broom as a piracy consultant after the book comes out. Ditto Music. It'll have to be Cable. Lots of resentment to feed off. A how-to book. Who'll publish it? The mainstream cowards won't touch it. What the hell are these people clapping for now? Maybe I'll self-publish and astroturf a story about being oppressed by Big Media. The idiots at the news aggregators always fall for that. Need to post a fake review on Slashdot. That works like a house on fire for O'Reilly. Position it as a gift that under-30s can give to their clueless parents. Maybe I'll get sued and the whole thing will go Streisand. Some geezer singing. What the? You've Got a Friend in Me? Let me out.

2 Understanding BitTorrent

BitTorrent is the most popular communications protocol (set of standard rules) that pirates use to exchange files over the internet. You can use the internet your whole life knowing nothing about its many protocols, but it pays to learn the basics of BitTorrent. (Don't confuse BitTorrent the protocol with BitTorrent the company—the latter founded by Bram Cohen, inventor of the protocol.)

Client-Server Networks

When you visit a typical website and click a link to download a (non-BitTorrent) file, you're using traditional **client-server** file distribution. The browser on your computer (the **client**) tells the **server** (the remote system holding the desired file) to transfer a copy of the file to your computer. As the download progresses, sequential pieces of the file travel over the internet and are assembled into a whole file on your drive at completion. The protocol handling the transfer is usually HTTP (Hypertext Transfer Protocol) or FTP (file transfer protocol). This scheme works well in general but has a few problems:

- You depend solely on the file's original distributor (a **single point of failure**)—if the server stalls, you can't download.

- Popular downloads are prone to bottlenecks as more and more people try to suck files from a single source. (Technically, the client-server approach doesn't **scale**.)

- The more popular the download, the more it costs the server in bandwidth charges.

- If the client or server has a problem mid-download (a power outage, lost connection, or system crash), then you're stuck with an incomplete file and typically must restart the download—possibly a big download—from scratch.

Peer-to-Peer Networks

Adequate mirroring (use of cloned servers) alleviates some of the problems of client-server networks, but BitTorrent solves them outright by using a **peer-to-peer** (**P2P**) file-sharing network. Unlike a server-based network, where most of the resources lie with a few central servers, a P2P network has only **peers**, which are ordinary computers (like yours) that all act as equal points on the network. Every machine on a P2P network can simultaneously download from and upload to every other machine, so the notion of dedicated clients and servers doesn't apply to P2P.

What You'll Need

To download files via BitTorrent, you need:

- A high-speed internet connection such as DSL, cable, fiber, T1, or satellite. BitTorrent is about transferring *big* files, but if you're downloading a small document or photo, a dial-up connection will work in a creaky sort of way.

- A computer running a mainstream operating system. This book covers Windows 7 and Mac OS X 10.6 (Snow Leopard).

- A free program called a BitTorrent client, described in Chapter 6.

- A hard drive with lots of free space.

When you visit a pirate website for the first time, you might be surprised by the massive amount and variety of what's freely available and the human motivations behind it. People share files to be generous, share knowledge, spread propaganda, return favors, sabotage employers, spread viruses, refute reputations, show technical prowess, advertise products, compete with other sharers, sell services, escape obscurity, be useful to others, betray friends, defy authority, show off to girls, earn bragging rights, and on and on.

Despite its strictureless amorality, the world of mass piracy has rules. (Rules emerge in all self-organizing complex systems.) Experienced file-sharers:

- Use filenames and keywords that make it easy for others to find the files.

- Organize multiple-file downloads in folders.

- Encode files in popular and standard formats such as MP3 for audio files and PDF or EPUB for books.

- Split different categories of files into independent distributions (movies, music, books, games, and so on).

With experience, you'll notice other rules, self-enforced because no one wants to look like a tourist. Individual pirate sites have their own rules (some forbid porn, for example) that they enforce by removing offending files or banning violators.

BitTorrent, Step by Step

Let's look at the birth, life, and decline of a generic file shared via Bit-Torrent. As a new pirate, you'll be downloading files that other people have provided. The first step below is something you do yourself only when you're sharing your own files with others. Any number of files can be shared in a single download, but for simplicity this example uses only one file.

One seeder. The original sharer uses his BitTorrent client to create a **torrent file** and save it on his hard drive. This file contains **metadata**, or information *about* the file to share, not the file itself. A torrent file:

- Has a filename that describes what's being shared, so that people can search for it. The filename for a TV show, for example, should contain at least the show's title and episode number.

- Has the filename extension .torrent (for details about extensions, Chapter 3).

- Points to the location (path) on the sharer's hard drive of the file to share.

- Specifies a **tracker** to manage file sharing. A tracker is a server but not in the sense used in a client-server network. That is, it's not a central location that holds the file but a traffic cop that directs the connections of everyone who's transferring (downloading or uploading) the shared file. Trackers can negotiate huge numbers of connections; it's common for tens of thousands of people to transfer the same movie at the same time. The sharer can choose from among many public (open) and private trackers run by pirate websites.

- Contains other metadata, such as filenames, file sizes, and error-checking values (checksums).

- Is small, about 20 KB. If you're curious, you can open a torrent file in a text editor, but its contents are encoded for compactness.

The sharer then uploads the torrent file to a pirate website (not necessarily the same site whose tracker he's using) and types a title and description full of searchable keywords. The tracker adds the **torrent** to its pool, then the site indexes it and gives it its own webpage and download link.

The nascent torrent now waits for people to notice and download it. The original sharer is, for now, the torrent's only seeder. A **seeder** is a peer who has an entire copy of a file and offers it for upload. In a torrent's early stages, the initial seeder can't turn off his computer, as this would make the complete file unavailable. Nor can he edit, rename, delete, or move the shared file on his drive, which would corrupt the torrent.

One seeder/one leecher.   You find the torrent (see Chapter 8), click its link in your browser, and then open the torrent file in your BitTorrent client. The download starts as the file travels, slowly at first, over the network from the original seeder's hard drive to yours. You're now a **leecher**: a peer who doesn't have the entire file and is downloading it. Peers (seeders and leechers) sharing the same torrent are called a **swarm**. A file distributed via BitTorrent is broken into many equal-sized **pieces**, like the cars of a freight train. These pieces are sent randomly—not sequentially—to a swarm's leechers.

One seeder/two leechers.   Time passes. It's just the two of you, seed and leech. You've downloaded most of the file but are still missing pieces. Then a new leecher joins the swarm and starts downloading the file. And here's where BitTorrent changes the game: the file pieces of *everyone* in a swarm — seeders and leechers alike — are available to everyone else in the swarm. So the new leecher downloads pieces from not only the original seeder but from *you* too, even though you don't yet have the entire file. Now you're simultaneously downloading pieces from the original seeder and uploading pieces to the new leecher. In a short time, the other leecher will get random pieces from the original seeder that you don't yet have, and he will start uploading to you too. Contrast this scheme with that of a client-server network, where clients can't communicate with each other and can get pieces from only the server.

Two seeders/many leechers.   You finish downloading the file and the torrent gains steam as new leechers join the swarm. You've transformed from leecher to seeder now that you have the entire file, meaning you're no longer downloading, only uploading to leechers. To everyone else in the swarm, you're now no different from the original seeder.

You now can delete the torrent file and do what you want with the file that you've downloaded. But quitting early is impolite, so seed for a few more hours (or days). BitTorrent works best when people continue to seed *after* their downloads finish. When seeding, you can open or copy the files that you've downloaded but if you edit, rename, delete, or move them, they become unavailable to the swarm. Uploading is much slower than downloading (typically, about one tenth the speed), so seeding won't dent your bandwidth, particularly in large swarms.

Usage note: Originally, *leecher* referred to someone who downloaded much more than he uploaded. Most BitTorrent sites now use the term neutrally but in some contexts *leecher* still denotes selfishness and *peer* is the neutral term.

Many seeders/many leechers.   The swarm grows large as new leechers join and old leechers become seeders. Now any peer can shut down his computer or quit the swarm without affecting the other peers. If a leecher quits, he can resume downloading later at the point where he left off. Even the initial seeder can quit the swarm now that so many other seeders exist. The tracker manages connections and traffic-flow as peers come and go.

Few seeders/few leechers.   Over time, the torrent declines as seeders leave the swarm. A torrent's life span can be hours or years, depending on its popularity and the conduct of its seeders. Other things equal, the more a swarm shrinks, the longer it takes to complete a download. Swarms with only a handful of peers can be quite slow.

Death.   A torrent with no seeders is **dead** but can be revived if someone **reseeds** by rejoining the swarm as a seeder to allow the remaining leechers to complete their downloads. Torrent listings show the current number of seeders and leechers (zero seeders = dead). Some pirate websites exclude dead torrents from search results by default.

If a torrent dies while you're still downloading, don't just delete it from your BitTorrent client. Wait a few days to see whether a reseeder appears. If a torrent dies just before you've completed downloading a file, you may be able to get the missing pieces from the swarm's other leechers. If so, it's courteous to stay on as a seeder. If not, you're out of luck unless you can get the same file from a different torrent or an alternative source like RapidShare (*rapidshare.com*). Megaupload (*megaupload.com*), or Usenet.

Now you know how BitTorrent works. A few more points:

- In contrast to this slow-motion example, the genesis of real-life torrents is often rapid. Newly released torrents for popular TV shows and movies swell to thousands of leechers in minutes. BitTorrent easily handles such flashcrowds.

- You might prefer to think of the pieces of a file as pages of a book or nucleotides of a DNA strand (rather than cars of a freight train) because pieces must be reassembled *in their proper order* for the information to keep its integrity.

- You can't choose whom you trade pieces with. BitTorrent clients enforce tit-for-tat trading by monitoring peers and choking leechers who try to game bandwidth.

- Your personal files are safe. BitTorrent restricts swarm access to only the shared files on your drive. Despite millions of savvy users, no fatal security flaw has come to light.

- To see BitTorrent in action, visit *mg8.org/processing/bt.html*.

3

File Types

Understanding file types lets you:

- Predict and control what happens when you double-click files that you've downloaded.

- Recognize unexpected or unfamiliar files in suspicious torrents. For example, an executable file bundled with a movie, music, photo, or book torrent should raise a red flag.

- Save time and bandwidth. By scanning the file list in a movie torrent, you can choose to download only the video file and exclude inessentials like subtitle, readme, snippet, screenshot, and spam files.

You should already know how to install and run programs, manage your files and folders, and change control-panel settings.

About File Types

Windows and OS X use the same file-type mechanism. When you double-click a Word document, your system launches Microsoft Word with that document open. It launches Word—rather than, say, your browser or Photoshop—because a document's **file type**, or **file format**, is embedded in its filename, as the (usually three) characters appearing after the name's last dot. These characters, called an **extension** or **filename extension**, link a document to a program. The link between a file type and its default program is an **association**. For example, the extension of the file readme.txt is .txt, denoting a plain-text file that will open in your text editor (Notepad, TextEdit, or whatever text editor you've specified). The extension of my.novel.doc is .doc, which tells your OS that the file is a document in the Microsoft Word file format. (Words in long filenames are generally separated by spaces, dots, or hyphens.)

Most files found on pirate sites use common formats and extensions. These formats, and their associated programs, are explained where they're relevant. Some notable ones are:

- .avi, .mkv, and .mp4 for movies, TV shows, and videos

- .jpg and .png for photos, artwork, and pictures

- .mp3 for music and audio books

- .pdf, .epub, and .mobi for books, magazines, and documents

- .txt, .nfo, .rtf, and .html for plain or formatted text

- .cbr and .cbz for comic books

- .otf and .ttf for fonts

- .iso, .cue/.bin, and .dmg for disk images

- .url for links to webpages (usually spam)

It's easy to set the default program for all files of the same type. You can change the program that opens all your digital photos from Picasa to Photoshop, for example, without having to change any .jpg files. If a newly installed program hijacks an association to become a file type's unwelcome default, you can reverse the change. (This misbehavior is less common than it used to be; now, installers usually let you manually set a program's associations.)

It may seem odd that the ability to open a file depends partially on something as easy to mistype as its filename, but when you rename a file in Windows or OS X, its name is selected only up to the last dot, letting you type a new name without accidently changing the extension. If you *do* edit the extension, you're prompted to confirm the change. Changing an extension won't alter the file's contents or format, but it will change how the OS interacts with the file. Renaming a webpage file from index.html to index.txt, for example, causes the file to open by default in your text editor instead of your browser.

Hidden Extensions

Windows and OS X hide filename extensions by default, which is why the file Kauai.jpg appears as only Kauai in a folder or on the desktop. Extension-hiding may make your screen look friendlier, but it also forces you to discern a file's type from its (possibly tiny) icon or the containing folder's (possibly invisible) Type or Kind column. Instead of seeing merely LoveLetter, show extensions to see LoveLetter.avi (a movie), LoveLetter.pdf (a book), or LoveLetter.exe (a virus?) and anticipate which program will launch when you open the file.

Unregistered Extensions

OSes come with a list of **registered** filename extensions for built-in programs. When you install a new program, it registers its own extensions. The default program for .jpg files, for example, on a fresh copy of Windows is Windows Photo Viewer (in OS X, it's Preview). Install Microsoft Excel and it registers itself as the default program for .xls and .xlsx files, among others.

If you double-click a file that has an unregistered extension, you're prompted to specify a compatible program. To find file types, extensions, and programs, go to *fileinfo.com* or read Wikipedia's list of file formats at *en.wikipedia.org/wiki/list_of_file_formats*. Files that have no extension are usually text files containing release notes or support files not meant to be opened (support files display as random-looking garbage in a text editor).

Windows Tasks

Windows maintains a master list that pairs each filename extension with its default program. A file's Properties window shows its file type and associated program (and other metadata). You can override the default program for specific files.

To open a file's Properties window:

Do any of the following:

- Right-click the file and choose Properties from the shortcut menu. (The Properties command is usually at the bottom of the menu.)

- Select the file and choose File > Properties.

- Select the file, hold down the Alt key, and then press Enter.

- Hold down the Alt key and double-click the file.

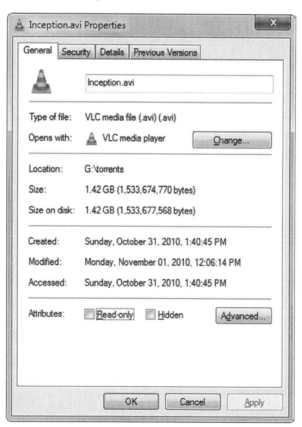

To show or hide filename extensions for all files:

1   Open the Start menu and choose Control Panel > Appearance and Personalization > Folder Options.

   or

   In Windows Explorer, click Organize on the toolbar and choose Folder and Search Options.

   or

   Open the Start menu, type *folder options* in the Search box, and then press Enter.

2   In the Folder Options window, click the View tab, turn on or off "Hide extensions for known file types," and then click OK.

   Note: If a filename has an unregistered extension, Windows shows the complete name even if extension-hiding is turned on.

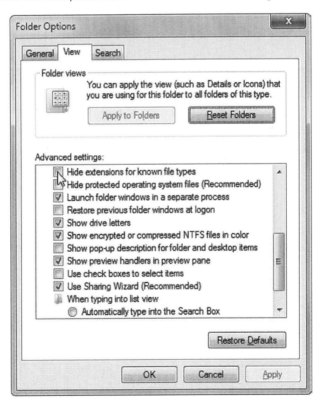

To open a specific file with a nondefault program:

1 Right-click the file, choose the desired program from the Open With submenu, and skip the remaining steps.

   or

   If the desired program isn't listed in the Open With submenu, choose Open With or Open With > "Choose default program."

2 In the Open With window, select the desired program (if it isn't listed, then click Browse and select it).

3 Turn off "Always use the selected program to open this kind of file."

4 Click OK.

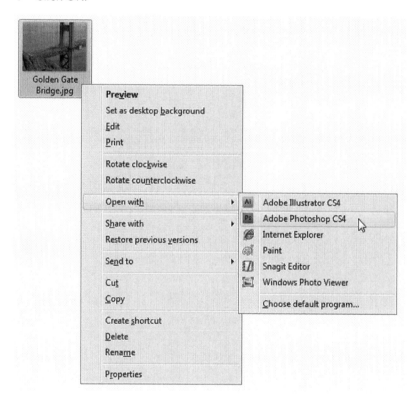

To change the default program for all files of a specific file type by using a file:

1 Right-click any file of the target file type and, from the short-cut menu, choose Open With or Open With > "Choose default program."

2 In the Open With window, select the new default program (if it isn't listed, then click Browse and select it).

3 Turn on "Always use the selected program to open this kind of file."

4 Click OK.

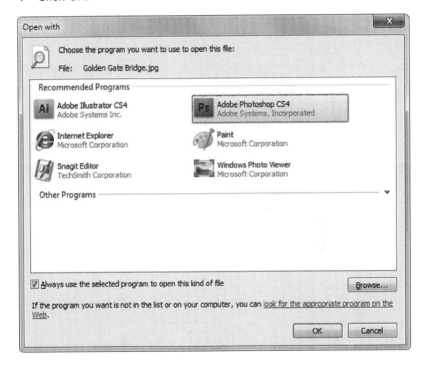

To change the default program for all files of a specific file type by using the program:

1   Open the Start menu, type *default* in the Search box, and then click "Set your default programs" (under Control Panel) in the results list.

or

Choose Start > Control Panel > Programs > Default Programs > "Set your default programs."

2   In the Set Default Programs window, select the new default program.

3   Do one of the following:

• To set the program as the default for *every* file type that it can open, click "Set this program as default." For example, you can set a media player to open all your video and audio files.

• To set the program as the default for *some* file types, click "Choose defaults for this program," turn on the checkboxes for the desired file types, and then click Save.

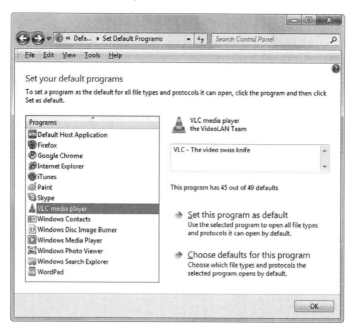

To change the default program for all files of a specific file type by using the filename extension:

1 Open the Start menu, type *associated* in the Search box, and then click "Change the file type associated with a file extension" (under Control Panel) in the results list.

   or

   Choose Start > Control Panel > Programs > Default Programs > "Associate a file type or protocol with a program."

2 In the Set Associations window, select the filename extension in the list, and then click "Change program."

3 In the Open With window, select the new default program (if it isn't listed, then click Browse and select it).

4 Click OK and then Close.

To open a file that has an unregistered extension (or no extension):

1   Double-click the mystery file.

2   Do one of the following:

- If you don't know which program can open the file, click "Use the Web service to find the appropriate program" to try to look up the extension on Microsoft's website. If Microsoft draws a blank, refer to one of the websites listed in "Unregistered Extensions" earlier in this chapter.

- To open the file in a program that's installed on your computer, click "Select the program from a list of installed programs," select a compatible program in the Open With window, and then turn on "Always use the selected program to open this kind of file" if you want.

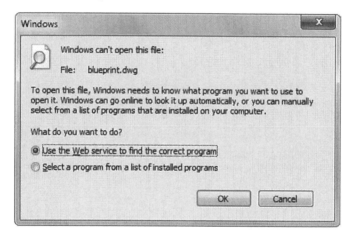

OS X Tasks

OS X maintains a master list that pairs each filename extension with its default program. A file's Info window shows its file type and associated program (and other metadata). You can override the default program for specific files.

To open a file's Info window:

Do any of the following:

- Right-click (or Ctrl-click) the file and choose Get Info from the shortcut menu.

- Select the file and choose File > Get Info or press Command+I.

  Note: These actions also work when multiple files are selected.

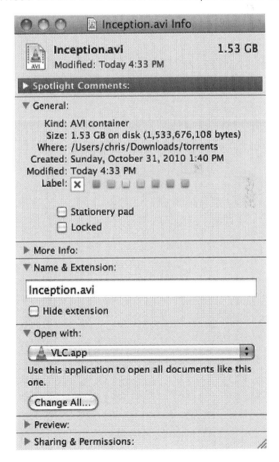

To show or hide the filename extension for a specific file:

1 Right-click (or Ctrl-click) the file and choose Get Info from the shortcut menu.

2 In the Name & Extension section of the Info window, turn on or off "Hide extension."

To show or hide filename extensions for all files:

1 In Finder, choose Finder > Preferences or press Command+, (comma).

2 In the Preferences window, click the Advanced pane and turn on or off "Show all filename extensions."

Note: Some filename extensions (such as those of imported photos) will show even if extension-hiding is turned on.

To show or suppress warnings when you change a file's extension:

1 In Finder, choose Finder > Preferences or press Command+, (comma).

2 In the Preferences window, click the Advanced pane and turn on or off "Show warning before changing an extension."

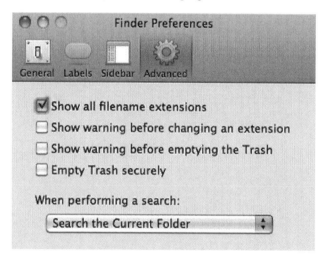

To open a specific file with a nondefault program:

Do any of the following:

- Right-click (or Ctrl-click) the file and choose Open With from the shortcut menu.

- Select the file and choose File > Open With.

- Select the file, click ✿ on the toolbar, and then choose Open With.

- Drag the file onto the program's icon in Finder or the Dock.

- Open the program that you want to use, choose File > Open, and then locate the file.

  Note: If the program isn't listed in the Open With menu, choose Other to locate it.

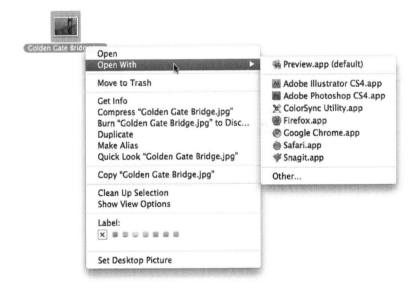

To change the default program for a specific file:

Do any of the following:

- Hold down the Option key, right-click (or Ctrl-click) the file, and then choose Always Open With from the shortcut menu.

- Select the file, hold down the Option key, and then choose File > Always Open With.

- Select the file, hold down the Option key, click ⚙ on the toolbar, and then choose Always Open With.

- Select the file, choose File > Get Info (or press Command+I), and then choose a program from the "Open with" drop-down list. (Don't click Change All.)

- If multiple files are selected, hold down the Option key, choose File > Show Inspector (or press Option+Command+I), and then select a program from the "Open with" drop-down list.

  Note: If the program isn't listed in the Always Open With menu, choose Other to locate it.

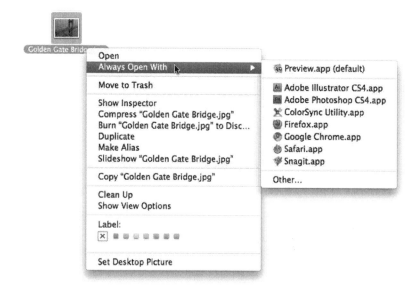

To change the default program for all files of a specific file type:

1 Select any file of the target file type.

2 Choose File > Get Info (or press Command+I).

3 In the Info window, choose a new default program from the "Open with" drop-down list or choose Oher to locate a different program.

4 Click Change All.

To open a file that has an unregistered extension (or no extension):

1 Double-click the mystery file.

2 Click Choose Application, select a compatible program in the Choose Application window, and then click Open. If you draw a blank, refer to one of the websites listed in "Unregistered Extensions" earlier in this chapter.

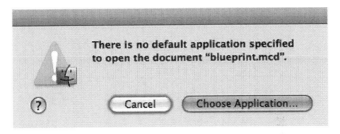

There is no default application specified to open the document "blueprint.mcd".

(?)   Cancel   Choose Application...

4 Malware

File-sharing networks are infested with nasty bits of software that will wreak havoc with your computer and perhaps your well-being. If you're thinking "My kid takes care of that," "That's a background task for my computer" or "I own a Mac," then you lack healthy paranoia.

About Malware

Malicious software, or **malware**, includes viruses, spyware, adware, trojan horses, worms, and rootkits, whose attacks range from mild (slowing your machine) to irritating (spewing pop-up ads or crashing your system) to transforming (destroying your data or stealing your identity). Some malware conceals itself. If your PC is a malware-infected **zombie**, it secretly obeys a remote server, typically sending spam in the background by using your bandwidth and processor. (A collection of zombies is a **botnet**, which third parties can rent from the infector for spam campaigns, remote attacks, or click fraud.)

Malware spreads via email attachments, networks, USB flash drives, rogue antimalware programs, and websites that push installable "add-ins." Pirates are threatened mainly by malicious links and infected files.

Malicious Links

A poker-book torrent has no reason to contain but one file: the book. But some payloads also contain links to no-name poker rooms, dodgy rakeback programs, online casinos, and other places best avoided. Such links, which can be part of any torrent, come as separate URL (.url), MHTML (.mht, .mhtml), or HTML (.html, .htm) files. Double-clicking one of these internet shortcuts opens your browser to a particular webpage. These links almost always lead to spammy, crooked, useless, or for-pay sites. And you risk a **drive-by download**: malware that exploits browser security holes to secretly self-install when you simply *visit* a website. Fortunately, these threats can be easily sidestepped:

- If the links come as separate files, turn them off when you first open the torrent (see Chapter 10).

- If the links are bundled in an archive (.rar or .zip file), download the archive and extract only the files of interest (see Chapter 5).

- If a password-protected archive requires that you visit a website to get the password, don't visit the site. Either delete the download or, if your alarm bells aren't ringing, scan the torrent's user comments for the password (see Chapter 10).

- If you're unsure about a link file (say, instructions.url or readme.html), open it in a text editor rather than in your browser.

Infected Files

Download and double-click the wrong file, and you're infected. Wary beginners have rules of thumb to protect them:

- Text files that don't contain scripts are always safe.

- Video, picture, and audio files are rarely unsafe.

- PDF and HTML files can *link* to malicious code. PDF and CHM files can also be infected with malicious code (but usually aren't).

- The default security settings for Microsoft Office stop macro viruses embedded in Word (.doc, .docx), Excel (.xls, .xlsx), and PowerPoint (.ppt, .pptx) documents.

- Applications, games, screen savers, scripts, key generators, cracks, disk images, and other executable files are where danger lies. Application-support files (.dll, .vbx, .vxd) can also be dangerous.

- Popular torrents aren't a threat (hundreds of savvy peers quickly spot subterfuge).

- Lots of piracy groups, identified by their aliases, have popular reputations for providing safe, quality downloads.

- Pirate sites let users post comments about torrents and flag their quality.

- Antimalware false positives result in often-ignorable user comments like "This torrent has a trojan horse."

Vigilance

These rules soon will coalesce to a *feel* for suspicious torrents. It's a step toward vigilance. The only way to protect yourself online is to act like everything on the internet is a scam; that people are always trying to trick and rob you by playing on your ignorance, loneliness, greed, empathy, guilt, or stupidity.

True vigilance is rare in cultures grounded in the idea that people don't have to live with the consequences of their actions. But humans are built to be vigilant. You see it in soldiers, pilots, loggers, athletes, cops, roofers, and hunters. It kept your ancestors from being shredded by lions, and keeps your kids from being pounded by bullies. Online, threats abound:

- Microsoft didn't take security seriously until Windows Vista in 2006 (far too late).

- At this writing, no viable Mac OS X malware has emerged. But Apple issues security updates regularly, so weakness is there should malware writers attack.

- The web was designed to be open (specifically, to share academic research). Implementations for banking and other secure transactions are bolted to an architecture made for sharing.

- Data and executable code occupy contiguous memory (that is, they share the same address space). This security hole lets code self-modify and lets data execute as code, permitting common and destructive code injection attacks.

- Other offenders: unauthenticated email, WEP, ActiveX controls, permissive C compilers, null-terminated strings, Flash cookies, evercookies, unencrypted IP packets, plaintext passwords, FTP, backward compatibility, security through obscurity, statelessness, invalid certificates, and misleading user interfaces.

Prevention

The best way to avoid malware is to *behave* safely and develop a sense of what the real risks are. A few tips:

Operating system. Use the current release of your OS and keep it updated with the latest security patches. Always update immediately. Windows and OS X auto-update by default. Don't use Windows XP — Microsoft's XP security updates have become rarer over time.

Programs. Uninstall any old versions of your software and keep the latest versions up to date. Programs usually let you update from the Help menu, the Options or Preferences dialog box, or (in OS X) the application menu.

Firewall. A firewall is a gatekeeper that can block internet traffic, usually based on its source or destination. Windows and OS X have built-in firewalls that are turned on by default. Your router/modem probably has its own firewall and network address translation (NAT) enabled by default, protecting even ancient OSes from outside threats. (Not sure? Ask a geek.) Third-party software firewalls often cause problems with BitTorrent clients.

Wireless network. Change your router's default password and enable WPA or WPA2 security (don't use now-compromised WEP security).

Filename extensions. Always show them (see Chapter 3). If extensions are hidden, the file love-letter-for-you.txt.vbs appears without the .vbs, looking like a harmless text file while actually carrying a hostile Visual Basic script. Millions opened this file in 2000, infecting themselves and millions more via email with the ILOVEYOU worm, forever convincing system administrators that ordinary users will click anything. Even with extensions showing, the file

FreeMP3s.txt   .exe

will appear to be harmless if the embedded spaces hide the .exe extension in a narrow column.

Browser. Browse with Mozilla Firefox (*mozilla.com/firefox*), not Internet Explorer or Safari. Use Firefox's Adblock Plus, FlashBlock, and Better-Privacy extensions. More-advanced users can look at NoScript. Other privacy and security extensions are at *addons.mozilla.org*.

Hosts file. Instead of using a browser extension, you can use a hosts file to block ads and third-party cookies. A hosts file is a text file that doesn't use system resources and isn't browser-dependent. Try *mvps. org/winhelp2002/hosts.htm* or *hosts-file.net*.

Education. Read Wikipedia's article about social engineering at *en.wikipedia.org/wiki/Social_engineering_(security)*. For current threats, read RISKS Digest (*catless.ncl.ac.uk/risks*) and Bruce Schneier's Crypto-Gram Newsletter (*schneier.com*). For Windows-specific threats, visit Microsoft Security at *microsoft.com/security*. Browse through the lectures at the Chaos Communication Congress (*events.ccc.de*).

Backups. If you back up an infected file, it'll reinfect you when you restore it to your computer.

Ads. Never click them, including those disguised as "sponsored results."

Passwords. Use a different password for each account. Write them down or use a program like Password Safe (*passwordsafe.sourceforge. net*). Cormac Herley (*research.microsoft.com/en-us/people/cormac*) writes critically of common password advice; for starters, try "So Long, And No Thanks for the Externalities" and "Do Strong Web Passwords Accomplish Anything?"

Antimalware. Don't use it.

Antimalware

That's right. Don't use it. Like a gated community, antimalware makes you no safer and may prompt you to take *more* risks through a false sense of security (the Peltzman effect). Vigilant pirates are paranoids who don't use antimalware and yet rarely, if ever, get infected.

Antimalware publishers can't keep up with the enormous number of malware variants in the wild, and independent tests show low rates of malware recognition (even for malware hidden by rudimentary techniques). Still, if you notice suspicious disk, network, desktop, or browser activity, scan your machine for malware. For Windows, try Microsoft Security Essentials, Avast, and Kaspersky (in tandem if necessary). For other OSes and products, read Wikipedia's list of antivirus programs at *en.wikipedia.org/wiki/List_of_antivirus_software*. If an infection or threat is recognized, it's deleted or quarantined; otherwise, you must wait for a fix, hire a geek, reinstall your OS, or live with the infection.

Antimalware programs tend to be bloated resource-suckers that increase startup and load times, and assert themselves throughout your workspace. Their frequent warnings, self-updates, and pop-up messages will interfere with your workflow, program installations, routine internet transactions, and peace of mind. But they're popular BitTorrent downloads, so pirates do use them. If you use one, keep in mind that its barrage of cry-wolf warnings will eventually cause you to regard all warnings as false positives, and you'll blandly click "Yes" when a real threat finally comes along. Also, antimalware often causes problems with BitTorrent clients (Chapter 6). In my brief tests, Microsoft Security Essentials was easiest to live with; it's free via Windows Update or at *microsoft.com/security_essentials*.

A few more tips:

- Antimalware is popularly called "antivirus software," a term too specific for marketers, who say "internet security suite."

- Media files (movies, photos, music, and so on) are almost always benign. The Bloodhound.Exploit.13 trojan horse (2004), however, involved .jpg images and flaws in Windows, which have since been fixed. Even so, these types of threats are so unlikely that you're better off worrying about more-common vectors of infection.

- To turn off Windows antimalware alerts, open the Start menu, choose Control Panel > System and Security > Action Center > "Change Actions Center settings" (in the left pane), and then turn off the security messages for "Spyware and related protection" and "Virus protection."

- See also "Spotting Fakes" in Chapter 8.

5 Archives

If you've ever downloaded a .zip file or received one attached to an email message, then you have experience with archives. Pirates need more than the simple support that Windows and OS X have for archives.

About Archives

An **archive** is a collection of any number of files and folders compressed and combined into a single file. Compressing files reduces the space they occupy on drives and decreases the time they take to download, so it's common for people to share their files as archives. Common, but misguided. The formats used for video, picture, audio, application, game, book, disk-image, and almost every other type of file distributed over BitTorrent are *already* compressed, so archiving doesn't reduce download time and adds the extra step of decompressing after the download finishes. (You can't repeatedly compress a file to make it ever smaller; otherwise, you'd ultimately be able to compress all the world's data into a single byte.)

Archives also limit choice. A season of *24* distributed as a single archive file rather than as 24 separate video files forces you to download the entire archive rather than only the episodes you want (say, all but the middle 20 episodes). In fact, an archived media file is a yellow flag that the torrent's creator might be forcing you to download more than just the files of interest. Force-fed files are often spam, malware, or self-promotion in the form of small text, executable, or internet-shortcut files (see Chapter 4). Happily, you can extract only the files that you want from the archive and toss the rest without a glance.

Often, archives arrive split into smaller parts (one file per part), which are reassembled silently and automatically when you open the archive. Split archives are a holdover from the space-limited days of yore. Now, we have cheap terabyte drives, cloud storage, and filesystems that can accommodate monster files.

Archives also tend to shorten a torrent's life. After extracting an archive's original files, it's natural to delete the now-redundant archive. This loss makes it impossible to seed (or reseed) the torrent.

By fashion or inertia, archives remain part of piracy.

Types of Archives

Archives, like other classes of files, come in various formats. The most common file format used for torrents is **RAR**, followed distantly by **ZIP**. (In mainstream computing, ZIP is king and RAR is rare.) RAR beats ZIP as a compression format because it produces much smaller archives in about the same amount of time. When you finish downloading an archive, you **extract** copies of its original files to your drive, leaving the archive itself unchanged. Extracting is also called unarchiving or unpacking. Conversely, making an archive file is called archiving or packing. For ZIP archives, there's zipping and unzipping. You may encounter the odd torrent archived in **7Z**, **GZIP**, **TAR**, **SIT** (StuffIt), or another format. These archives are all extracted in the same way. In general, approach non-RAR and non-ZIP archives with caution.

Working with Archives

Windows and OS X have built-in support for ZIP but not for RAR, so you must install a **file archiver** to extract files. Wikipedia lists file archivers at *en.wikipedia.org/wiki/Comparison_of_file_archivers*. I use WinRAR (*win-rar.com*) for Windows and WinZip (*winzip.com*) for OS X. Popular open-source archivers include 7-Zip (*7-zip.org*) and IZArc (*izarc.org*). All work similarly and support RAR, ZIP, and other formats.

ZIP files have the filename extension .zip and RAR files have the extension .rar. If a RAR archive is split into parts, its filenames end in

.part01.rar, .part02.rar, .part03.rar, . . .

or

.rar, .r00, .r01, .r02, . . .

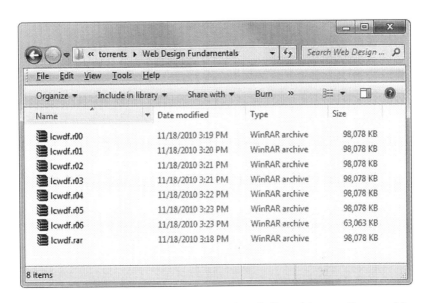

To open an archive file, double-click it. Split archives self-assemble in the file archiver, provided their parts all are in the same folder. If you double-click an .r00 file (or any .rnn file), your OS might complain that it doesn't know which program to use to open the file. To associate .rnn files with your file archiver, see Chapter 3. (WinRAR registers .rnn associations automatically on installation but most other archivers don't.)

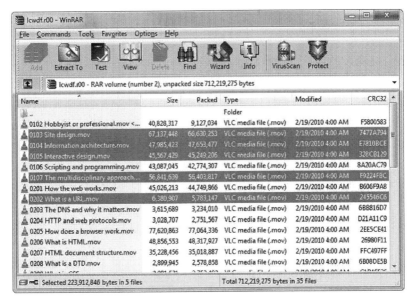

Archives work somewhat like folders in that they "contain" files, so archivers display an archive's contents like files listed in a Windows Explorer or Finder window. Your archiver's help system explains how to display, select, and extract files. The main operations are consistent across archivers:

- To extract files, select them in the archiver window (some archives contain only one file), click the Extract button, and then specify a destination folder. Extraction can take minutes for large archives.

- To select adjacent files in a list, click the first file and then either Shift-click the last file or press Shift+arrow key. To select nonadjacent files, Ctrl-click each file (or Command-click in OS X). To select all files, press Ctrl+A (or Command+A).

- Double-clicking a file in an archiver window opens it without copying it to your hard drive.

- You can drag files from an archiver window to the desktop or a folder window, where they auto-extract. Don't use this method if maintaining the files' original folder structure is important.

- Archivers can integrate with the shell, meaning that they can add commands to context menus in Windows Explorer or Finder. If you right-click an archive file and choose the "Extract Here" command, for example, the archive's complete contents are extracted without actually launching the file archiver. For security, always double-click an archive and inspect its files in an archiver window before extracting them.

- Some archives come with a separate **SFV** (.sfv) or **checksum** file, created by the archiver. SFV stands for Simple File Validator. You can open this file in a text editor and, with a bit of technical skill, use its contents to determine whether the files downloaded correctly. Don't bother: BitTorrent already takes care of file integrity by using its own checksums for each piece of a torrent. You can delete SFVs or omit them from your download altogether.

6

Installing a BitTorrent Client

A **client** is a program that can, among other things, download files. A web browser, for example, is a client that downloads and displays webpages. An email client (say, Microsoft Outlook or Apple Mail) lets you download and manage your mail. To download files via BitTorrent, you must install and configure a **BitTorrent client**. (In the broader context of networks, *client* refers to an entire computer; in this chapter, it's a specific piece of software.)

About BitTorrent Clients

Wikipedia lists BitTorrent clients at *en.wikipedia.org/wiki/Bittorrent_clients*. For Windows and OS X, I use µTorrent (*utorrent.com*), the most popular client. Other commonly used clients include Vuze (*vuze.com*), BitTorrent (*bittorrent.com*), and Transmission (*transmissionbt.com*). Lately, I've been experimenting with Tixati (*tixati.com*). All are free and some run on several operating systems. For basic tasks, mainstream clients work similarly—learn to drive one and you can drive the rest. This book's examples use µTorrent. (The "µ" is the lowercase Greek letter mu and here denotes the scientific prefix for "micro." For typographic ease, "µTorrent" goes by the name "uTorrent" on the web.)

Installing a Client

Installing a BitTorrent client is no different than installing other programs. To be sure that a client isn't infected with malware, download it only from the publisher's website, not some third-party site. Before installation, shut down any antimalware (antivirus) programs. Separate instructions for Windows and OS X installations follow.

To install μTorrent (Windows):

1   Go to *utorrent.com*, click the Download link, and then save the file utorrent.exe on your drive. (The site autodetects Windows.)

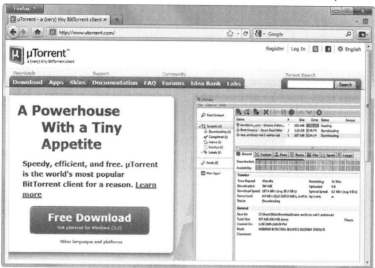

2   When the download completes, double-click torrent.exe and run the μTorrent Setup Wizard.

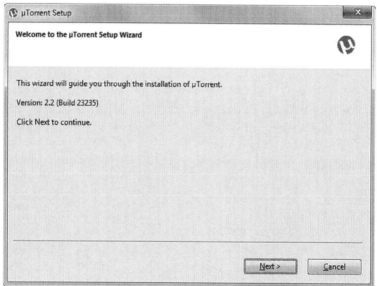

3 On the "Welcome to the µTorrent Setup Wizard" page, click Next.

4 On the "Warning" page, click Next.

5 On the "License Agreement" page, click I Agree.

6 On the "Choose Install Location" page, accept the default installation folder or click Browse to use or create a different location. If
   you like, turn off the Start-menu and icon checkboxes. Click Next.

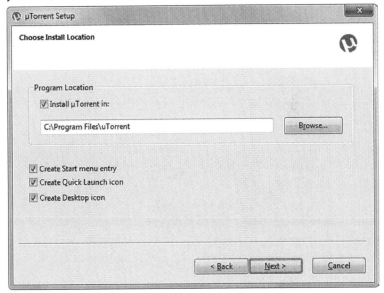

7 On the "Configuration" page, turn on "Add an exception for
   µTorrent in Windows Firewall" to let µTorrent communicate
   through Windows' built-in firewall. If you're using a third-party firewall, you must configure it separately.

   If you pay for internet service by the megabyte or if you don't
   plan to use µTorrent heavily, turn off "Start µTorrent when Windows starts up." (You can change this setting later in the Preferences window.)

8 On the "µTorrent Browser Bar Optional Installation" page, turn off
   all the checkboxes (all are spam options). Click Install.

   µTorrent registers itself as the default program for .torrent files
   and opens.

To install μTorrent (OS X):

1   Go to *utorrent.com*, click the Download link, and then save the disk image (.dmg file) on your drive. (The site autodetects OS X.)

2   When the download completes, double-click the .dmg file.

A disk icon appears on your desktop and the uTorrent window opens (if it doesn't open, double-click the disk icon).

3   In the uTorrent window, drag the uTorrent.app icon and drop it on the Applications icon.

μTorrent registers itself as the default program for .torrent files. To open μTorrent, click its icon in the Applications folder.

4   After installing μTorrent, you can delete the .dmg file and remove the disk icon from your desktop by dragging it to the Trash or right-clicking (or Ctrl-clicking) it and choosing Eject.

Getting Help

Before you start pirating, configure µTorrent to work with your particular system. Following the general instructions in this chapter will usually get you fast download speeds with µTorrent's default settings, but ekeing out every last bit per second depends on more factors than can be covered here, including your operating system, connection speed, latency, internet service provider (ISP), router, and firewall. If you need to troubleshoot, tweak, or better understand your configuration, try any of the following resources:

- Read the µTorrent help file, particularly the Setup Guide and Port Forwarding sections. In Windows, open µTorrent and choose Help > µTorrent Help (or press F1). In OS X, go to *utorrent.com/ documentation*, click "µTorrent Help File," and then download and extract the .chm file. To open .chm files in OS X, install a reader such as Chmox (*chmox.sourceforge.net*).

- Read the µTorrent FAQ (Frequently Asked Questions), particularly the Network section. Choose Help > µTorrent FAQ or go to *utorrent.com/faq*.

- Ask a question on the µTorrent forums. Choose Help > µTorrent Forums or go to *forum.utorrent.com*. Before posting your question, search the help file, FAQ, and forums to see whether it's been answered already, lest you be ignored or abused by the forums' participants.

- Search the web for *increase bittorrent speed* (or a similar phrase) and read articles by speed-obsessed pirates.

- Experiment. Change settings to find what works best for you.

- Hire someone. In most cases, a networking geek can get everything working (and explain the process) in less than two hours.

Limiting Upload Rates

Recall from Chapter 2 that BitTorrent requires all peers to simultaneously upload and download shared files. The top speed at which you can transfer data (up or down) depends on your bandwidth — the more you pay your ISP, the greater your bandwidth. Data speeds for DSL, cable, fiber, and other broadband connections let you download much faster than you can upload. This asymmetry arose because ordinary users generally receive (download) many more webpages, videos, pictures, messages, programs, and documents than they publish (upload).

Because too much outbound traffic can choke your download speed, you must **throttle**, or limit, µTorrent's maximum upload speed. In general, you don't have to throttle download speed. You can throttle upload rates automatically or manually.

To set the maximum upload rate automatically (Windows):

1 Quit all programs that access the internet, including browsers, mail/chat clients, antimalware, Skype, iTunes, and backup tools.

2 Open µTorrent and choose Options > Setup Guide or press Ctrl+G.

3 In the µTorrent Setup Guide, choose the location closest to you from the Bandwidth drop-down list. If a somewhat nearby place isn't listed, skip the remaining steps and set the upload rate manually, as described later in this section.

4 Click Run Tests and wait until the tests finish.

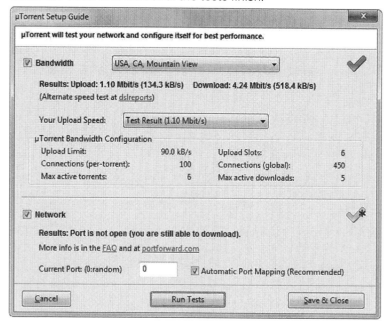

5 If the Bandwidth test succeeded, click Save & Close. If it failed, set the upload rate manually, as described later in this section.

If the Network test succeeded, click Save & Close. If it failed, check the resources listed in "Getting Help" earlier in this chapter and search for *firewall* or *router* or *port forwarding*.

To set the maximum upload rate automatically (OS X):

1 Quit all programs that access the internet, including browsers, mail/chat clients, antimalware, Skype, iTunes, and backup tools.

2 Open µTorrent.

3 Choose µTorrent > Preferences or press Command+, (comma).

4 In the Preferences window, click Bandwidth, and then turn on "Limit upload rate automatically."

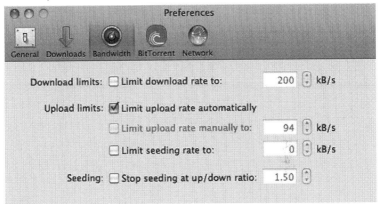

To set the maximum upload rate manually (Windows or OS X):

1 Quit all programs that access the internet, including browsers, mail/chat clients, antimalware, Skype, iTunes, and backup tools.

2 Open your browser and go to a website that can test broadband speeds. I use *speedtest.net* or *dslreports.com/speedtest*, but you can find others by searching the web for *speed test, bandwidth test, internet connection speed,* or a similar phrase. (Always run an independent speed test. *Don't* use the speeds that your ISP advertises.)

3 Run the test and note your upload speed. For more-accurate results, run the same test two or three times and calculate the average upload speed.

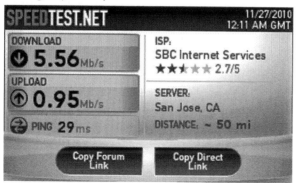

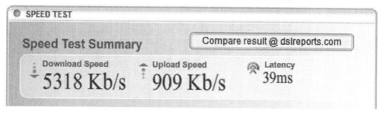

4 If necessary, convert the upload speed to kilobytes per second (KB/s).

Different sites report upload speeds in different units, such as megabits per second (Mb/s) or kilobits per second (Kb/s). The case of the letter "b" matters: an uppercase "B" means bytes and a lowercase "b" means bits. One byte = eight bits. If your upload speed is reported in KB/s, then use that number; otherwise, convert to KB/s by using one of the following formulas:

- To convert from Mb/s (megabits per second) to KB/s, multiply Mb/s by 128. For example, 0.95 Mb/s × 128 = 121.6 KB/s.

- To convert from Kb/s (kilobits per second) to KB/s, multiply Kb/s by 0.125. For example, 909 Kb/s × 0.125 = 113.6 KB/s.

- To convert from MB/s (megabytes per second) to KB/s, multiply Mb/s by 1024. For example, 0.115 MB/s × 1024 = 117.8 KB/s.

5 Multiply the upload speed by 0.8 and note the result (80% of capacity). For example, 117.8 KB/s × 0.8 = 94.2 KB/s.

6 Open μTorrent and do one of the following:

- In Windows, choose Options > Preferences (Ctrl+P) > Bandwidth (in the left pane) and set "Maximum upload rate (kB/s)" to the number that you calculated in the preceding step (rounded to the nearest whole number). Click OK.

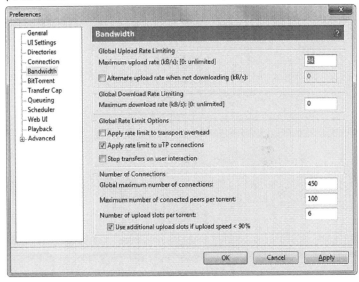

- In OS X, choose μTorrent > Preferences (Command+,) > Bandwidth, turn off "Limit upload rate automatically," turn on "Limit upload rate manually to," and then set the limit to the number that you calculated in the preceding step (rounded to the nearest whole number). Close Preferences.

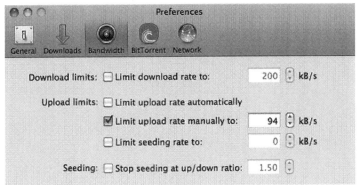

Other Settings

Though µTorrent's default configuration settings work fine in most cases, you can adjust them to suit you.

Limit download rates. If µTorrent is hogging bandwidth and slowing your browser, Skype calls, or other internet applications, you can do any of the following:

- Shut down µTorrent for a while.

- Limit the download rate. In Windows, choose Options > Preferences (Ctrl+P) > Bandwidth (in the left pane) and set "Maximum download rate (kB/s)." In OS X, choose µTorrent > Preferences (Command+,) > Bandwidth, turn on "Limit download rate to," and then set the download limit.

  Try a limit of 80%–95% your bandwidth's download capacity. To return to the maximum download speed, set the limit to zero (Windows) or turn off "Limit download rate to" (OS X).

- (Windows only) Throttle downloads on a schedule. Choose Options > Preferences (Ctrl+P) > Scheduler (in the left pane). Repeatedly click the boxes in the 24 x 7 grid to set hourly speed limits.

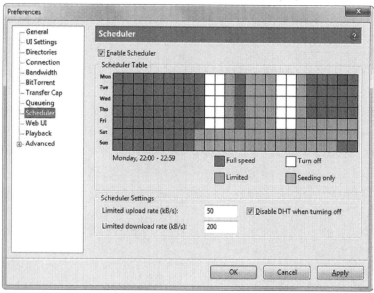

Adjust upload rates. If you followed the instructions in "Limiting Upload Rates" earlier in this chapter, then you limited your upload rate to about 80% of your bandwidth's upload capacity. If you adjust this rate, keep it within about 70%–80% of capacity or your download speed may suffer (either choked by µTorrent or swamped by outbound traffic).

Elude traffic shapers. Some ISPs engage in **traffic shaping**, intentionally blocking or throttling BitTorrent traffic (politics and money). If your ISP shapes traffic, then your BitTorrent downloads will progress more slowly than your normal (HTTP/FTP) downloads. The Vuze Wiki lists bad ISPs at *wiki.vuze.com/w/Bad_ISPs*. You can determine whether your ISP is throttling traffic by using the Max Planck Institute's Glasnost service at *broadband.mpi-sws.org/transparency*. The arms race between pirates and ISPs has left it hard to fool traffic shapers but a few basic countermeasures (short of switching ISPs) may help:

- Encrypt your BitTorrent traffic. In Windows, choose Options > Preferences (Ctrl+P) > BitTorrent (in the left pane) and set Outgoing Protocol Encryption to Enabled or Forced. In OS X, choose µTorrent > Preferences (Command+,) > BitTorrent and set Outgoing Encryption to Enable or Force. Forced encryption is the stronger setting.

- Use random BitTorrent ports. A **port** is a numbered tunnel for a certain kind of internet traffic. BitTorrent by default uses ports in the range 6881–6999 (typically port 6881). To keep traffic shapers guessing, you can randomize the port that µTorrent uses to listen for incoming connections. In Windows, choose Options > Preferences (Ctrl+P) > Connection (in the left pane) and turn on "Randomize port each start." In OS X, choose µTorrent > Preferences (Command+,) > Network and turn on "Randomize port during launch."

  Ports must be unfirewalled. Be sure that UPnP and NAT-PMP port mapping are turned on (their settings are near the Randomize setting). If you router doesn't support automatic port mapping, search for *port forwarding* in the resources listed in "Getting Help" earlier in this chapter.

Check firewall settings. You can make sure that your firewall has an exception allowing µTorrent traffic. In Windows, open the Start menu and choose Control Panel > System and Security > Windows Firewall > "Allow a program or feature through Windows Firewall" (in the left pane). In OS X, open the Apple menu and choose System Preferences > Security > Firewall > Advanced. For third-party firewalls, read the documentation.

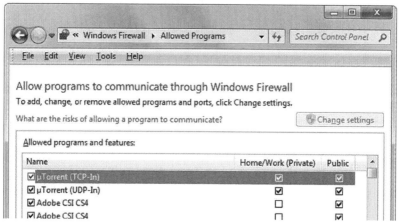

Check for updates. To be sure that you're using the latest version of µTorrent, check for updates automatically. In Windows, choose Options > Preferences (Ctrl+P) > General (in the left pane) and turn on "Check for updates automatically." In OS X, choose µTorrent > Preferences (Command+,) > General and turn on "Automatically check for updates."

Check connectivity at a glance. A color-coded network icon on the right side of the status bar indicates your connectivity. (The status bar runs along the bottom of the µTorrent window. To show it in Windows, choose Options > Show Status Bar or press F6.) A green icon means everything is OK. A persistent yellow icon or a red icon means a router or firewall problem. A clear icon means no torrents are active. Clicking the icon opens the Setup Guide (Windows) or Network Preferences (OS X). For details, open the µTorrent help file and search for *status bar*.

Try a different BitTorrent client. If you install a different BitTorrent client, it will register itself as the default program for .torrent files. In Windows, if don't want µTorrent to be your default client, choose Options > Preferences (Ctrl+P) > General (in the left pane) and turn off "Check association on startup" (for details about associations, see Chapter 3).

7 BitTorrent Search Engines

Start with large, well-maintained, active sites that have flourished despite legal and technical attacks:

- The Pirate Bay (*thepiratebay.org*)

- isoHunt (*isohunt.com*)

- btjunkie (*btjunkie.org*)

- KickassTorrents (*kickasstorrents.com*)

- ExtraTorrent (*extratorrent.com*)

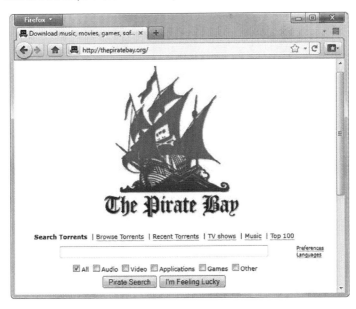

Finding BitTorrent Search Engines

No site is all-encompassing, so you may have to visit a few to find a torrent of interest. You'll eventually settle on your favorite sites and keep others in reserve for hard-to-find or special materials.

Sites come and go, and one day your favorite may go dark, block connections from your country, or be overrun with spam, malware, or ads. It's not hard to find BitTorrent search engines but keep in mind that file-sharing traffic, like most types of internet traffic, follows a power law (also called the 80-20 rule): only a few sites get the vast majority of pirate visits while the rest fight for scraps. Try any of the following methods to find sites:

- Read Wikipedia's comparison of BitTorrent sites at *en.wikipedia. org/wiki/Comparison_of_BitTorrent_sites*.

- Search the web for *file sharing news* or *torrent news* and scan articles for promising sites. Popular pirate news sites include TorrentFreak (*torrentfreak.com*), ZeroPaid (*zeropaid.com*), Slyck (*slyck.com*), and FileShareFreak (*filesharefreak.com*).

- Visit Alexa (*alexa.com*), a web traffic and ranking site, and search for *file sharing* or *bittorrent*. They list top file-sharing sites at *alexa.com/topsites/category/Top/Computers/Internet/ File_Sharing*.

- Search the web for *bittorrent sites*, *torrent search*, or a similar phrase. Don't trust "Top BitTorrent Sites" lists unless they quote traffic statistics from a legitimate source like Alexa, Quantcast, Compete, Nielsen, or Google DoubleClick.

- Find out who's being hassled. Reputable pirate sites are regularly sued or seized by trade groups and governments. Anti-piracy outfits go by initialisms: MPAA, RIAA, IFPI, CRIA, ICE, BPI, USCG, APB, and many more. Lawsuits usually fail to shut down sites and seizures only shift sites to different domains (web addresses). Scan the file-sharing news at the Electronic Frontier Foundation (*eff.org*), or visit Google News (*news.google.com*) and search for, say, *MPAA sues*.

- Search for BitTorrent sites in other languages, particularly Asian and European languages.

Features to Look For

First, browse the site's index. An **index** is a searchable list of .torrent files available for download. Sites index torrents uploaded by members or find torrents by using Google-style web crawlers. Some sites have specialized indexes for anime, live music, or nonpirated media. A site's chief benchmarks are its number of active users and daily number of new torrents indexed (and dead or fake torrents removed). The best sites provide timely, quality torrents and keep out spam, malware, and fakes by letting their users participate. Look for these features:

- Users can comment on or upvote/downvote torrents (crucial)

- Site operators or privileged users verify torrents as safe

- Frequent uploaders and release groups are rated by points-based or operator-validated reputation systems

- Private messaging, help chat, or user forums

- Few ads (use the Adblock and Flashblock browser extensions)

Metasearch Sites

A **metasearch** site doesn't compile its own index but searches other sites and aggregates the results. A Torrentz (*torrentz.com*) search, for example, returns a list of links to other BitTorrent search engines.

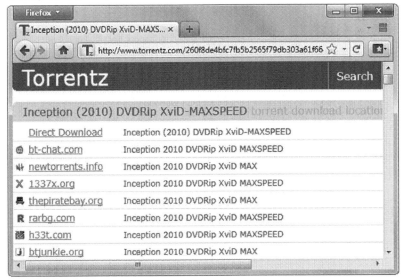

Private Sites

The BitTorrent sites in this chapter are **public** sites, meaning that anyone anytime can jump on, download, and then jump off—no registration required. **Private** sites, in contrast, have a limited number of memberships available during rare open-registration periods or via invitations from current members. These sites run their own trackers to better control content and keep out the riff-raff.

Private sites monitor each member's **share ratio**, which is the amount of data uploaded divided by the amount of data downloaded. Generous members have ratios greater than one, meaning that they've sent more data to other peers than they've received. Greedy, low-ratio members and bandwidth cheats can be booted off the site, memberships revoked. Thus, fear breeds long-lived torrents and high-speed downloads. Private sites are some of the best places to pirate and invitations can be hard to come by.

Private sites usually stonewall you with a login screen but Demonoid (*demonoid.me*) lets anyone, member or not, browse its torrents (though only members can actually download).

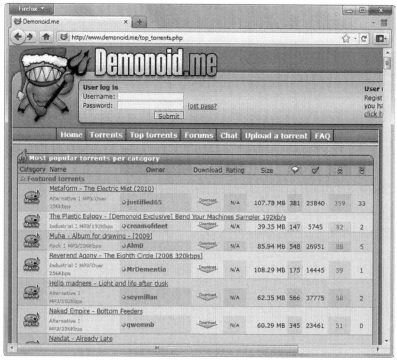

Google and Brethren

Google, Bing, Yahoo, Duck Duck Go, and other general search engines can find torrents. Type the name of what you're looking for followed by the word *torrent*. So common are pirate searches that often "torrent" is autosuggested as you type (Google no longer suggests piracy-related words in the US). The top results usually link to the dedicated BitTorrent sites listed earlier in this chapter.

Links to Torrents

Parties on all sides throw around terms like "BitTorrent website" and "linking" without defining them precisely. Copyright holders and their minions use these terms in the broadest sense, where simply *linking* to torrents is no different from providing copyrighted material. But most of the sites mentioned in this chapter are search engines that don't host their own tracker and consequently don't provide pirated content.

Their search results are no different from Google's except that they're restricted to torrents. Lawyers go after small fish because that's who they can shut down. They haven't sued Google because presumably even American courts wouldn't hold Google (or Bing or Yahoo) criminally liable for every search result.

In the US, Homeland Security's Immigration and Customs Enforcement (ICE) has, by using fatuous legal arguments at the behest of private interests, seized the domain names (web addresses) of several BitTorrent search engines that don't host content. These seizures won't affect piracy but they will skunk the .com top-level domain. BitTorrent search engines and other fringe businesses will migrate to domains perceived to be outside of US control. *Demonoid.com*, for example, is now *Demonoid.me* (the "me" stands for Montenegro).

8

Finding
Torrents

To find a torrent, go to a BitTorrent search engine (Chapter 7), type a search phrase in the Search box, and then press Enter. Search results are sorted by relevance and popularity (swarm size). Usually, one of the first few matches in the results list is the torrent you're looking for.

Search Tips

General search tips follow. For help with specific categories of torrents (movies, books, applications, and so on), refer to later chapters.

- To determine whether a torrent is relevant, Search compares the keywords in your search phrase to the name of the .torrent file, the names of the shared (content) files, and any title or description that the original seeder added. Words in filenames can be separated by spaces, dots, or hyphens; search engines treat them in the same way.

- Search boxes often have nearby filtering controls that can narrow a search or sort the results. Google-style operators can further narrow a search. To find an exact phrase, for example, enclose it in quotes (*"empire strikes back"*). Search engines vary in their support for search operators. For help, look for an Advanced Search, FAQ, or Help link on the site's home page.

- Click Browse to see all of a site's torrents, sorted by category or popularity.

- Click Recent (or Latest) to see a site's newest torrents, sorted by age or popularity.

- In any columnar list of torrents, click a column heading to sort by name, category, file size, age, swarm size, or a different measure. To reverse the sort, click the heading again.

- Some sites display a **search cloud** of the keywords used in that day's most-popular searches. In some clouds, the font size of keywords corresponds to the frequency of the search. Click any keyword to replicate the search.

  1080p 2010 2010 dvdrip 2010 dvdrip movies 2010 movies 2010 music 720p audio book axxo his bang theory bluray brrip burlesque burn notice christmas community despicable me dexter discography dvd dvdrip dvdrip 2010 ebook family guy faster fringe fxg games hindi hindi movies inception knight and day lil wayne movies movies 2010 movies 2010 dvdrip music music 2010 pc games r kelly r5 software t i tangled the league the office the town tv wii xbox 360

- Most sites have **RSS** feeds, which let you subscribe to a continually updated list of new torrents. Feeds can list all new torrents (like drinking from a firehose) or only certain categories of new torrents. RSS feeds are marked by orange icons 🔲 on the webpage or in the browser's address bar. To subscribe to a feed, click its icon. For details, search for *rss* in your browser's help system.

- Some torrents will appear as dead (no seeders) but it's possible the search engine isn't taking trackerless torrents into account. **Trackerless** torrents use the DHT (Distributed Hash Tracking) and PEX (Peer Exchange) protocols to dilute the need for a central tracker. Open a dead torrent and within minutes you may find peers via DHT or PEX. In µTorrent, DHT and PEX are turned on by default. To view or change these settings in Windows, choose Options > Preferences (Ctrl+P) > BitTorrent (in the left pane). In OS X, choose µTorrent > Preferences (Command+,) > BitTorrent.

- µTorrent, Vuze, and other BitTorrent clients have built-in Search that you can configure to work with your favorite search engines. In µTorrent for Windows, choose Options > Preferences (Ctrl+P) > Advanced (in the left pane) > UI Extras.

- BitTorrent search engines aren't the only places to get torrents. You can send or receive .torrent files via email or chat or download them via blog links.

Spotting Fakes

Antipiracy groups, scammers, and malware writers plant fake torrents, which can be downloads that never finish, unplayable videos, mislabeled files, or virus-carrying executables. Some fake-spotting tips:

- Delete any movie that requires you to download and install a rogue media player, like the trojan-laden 3wPlayer, DomPlayer, or x3 player. Be wary of videos that won't play in VLC media player (*videolan.org/vlc*). For details, see "Media Players" in Chapter 11.

- Delete any torrent that makes you visit a website to get a password, install a codec, or "activate" something.

- Don't download movie, music, picture, book or other media files packaged as or with executable (.exe) files.

- Suspect .rar and .zip archives (see Chapter 5) and .url files (see "Malicious Links" in Chapter 4). Many legitimate torrents have these files, but be vigilant nonetheless.

- Scan the torrent's user comments. Look for "Fake!" or queries about passwords or special media players. For popular torrents, comments like "Contains a trojan" can mostly be ignored as false positives from rookie pirates.

- Beware of heavily seeded torrents with few user comments. If a two-year-old movie has twenty thousand seeders, it's a fake.

- Avoid too-good-to-be-true torrents, like a DVD or Blu-ray copy of a movie seeded just as it premiers in theaters.

- Favor torrents released by organized piracy groups. Group aliases (MAXSPEED, aXXo, or EZTV, for example) are part of torrent names. Some sites flag trusted groups with special icons, foiling scammers who forge group names on fake torrents. VCDQ (*vcdq.com*) lists and rates group releases.

- Compare the size of the torrent to its description. The size of a two-hour .avi movie should between about 700 MB and 1.5 GB.

- Look for torrents that are verified as safe or high-quality by site operators or privileged users, or are heavily upvoted by ordinary users. Sites that verify torrents flag them with special icons.

- Some BitTorrent clients carry malware and are banned by various BitTorrent sites. Use one of the clients listed in Chapter 6.

- Download torrents from private sites, if possible, or popular public sites (Chapter 7) where fakes are more likely to be quickly spotted and removed.

- If you search for an approximate title, ignore results that mimic your search phrase. If you search for *indiana raiders ark movie*, stay away from any result that includes *indiana raiders ark movie* exactly.

- Never click a "sponsored" link.

Sponsored Results		
I'm a fake [FullVersion]	7295 downloads at 5396 kb/s	
I'm a fake - Full Download	8343 downloads at 6271 kb/s	
[HIGHSPEED] I'm a fake	8790 downloads at 4455 kb/s	
[TRUSTED DOWNLOAD] I'm a fake	8129 downloads at 6784 kb/s	

- (Advanced.) If you don't recognize a torrent's tracker, type or paste the tracker name into a general search engine (like Google). Fake trackers get few search results (which often contain "fake" or "spam"). Some fake trackers have names deceptively similar to those of well-known trackers.

- See also Chapter 4.

9

Customizing
Your Client

This chapter shows you how to set up the µTorrent interface in the way that I use it in this book's examples. After you download a few torrents, experiment and pick the settings that suit you.

User Interface

µTorrent for Windows offers more options than does the OS X version.

To customize the µTorrent user interface (Windows):

1   In µTorrent, choose Options > Preferences (Ctrl+P) > General (in the left pane).

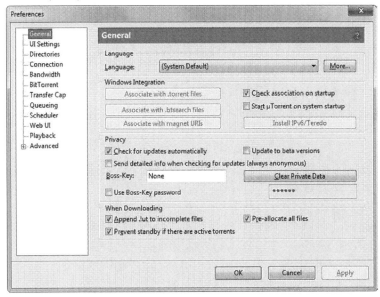

2 Turn on "Append .!ut to incomplete files."

This setting makes µTorrent append the filename extension .!ut to every content file that hasn't finished downloading. The file Avatar.avi is named Avatar.avi.!ut until the file is whole and .!ut is removed. Incomplete files appear as blank icons because .!ut isn't registered with a default program (see Chapter 3). A quick look in a folder window shows how many files are incomplete.

3 Turn on "Pre-allocate all files."

This setting makes µTorrent show the space reserved on your hard drive for all the content files that you select to download. This space equals the final size of the complete download, so files will appear to be huge even if you've downloaded only a small bit. As the download progresses, µTorrent "fills in" the allocated space with file pieces as they randomly arrive.

4 Click UI Settings (in the left pane).

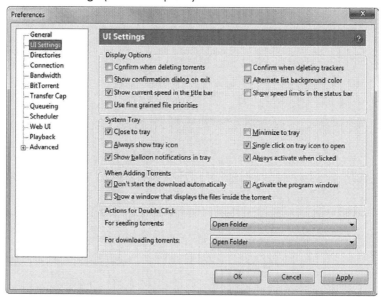

5 Turn on "Don't start the download automatically."

This setting prevents newly added torrents from starting automatically. After selecting which of the torrent's content files to download, you can start the torrent manually.

6   Turn on "Activate the program window."

This setting activates (makes frontmost) the µTorrent window when you add a new torrent.

7   Turn off "Show a window that displays the files inside the torrent."

This setting suppresses the Add New Torrent window when you add torrents. (Experienced pirates often turn *on* this setting to make custom changes to each new torrent.)

8   Choose Open Folder from the "For seeding torrents" and "For downloading torrents" drop-down lists.

Double-clicking an item in the torrent list opens the folder containing that torrent's content files.

9   Click Directories (in the left pane).

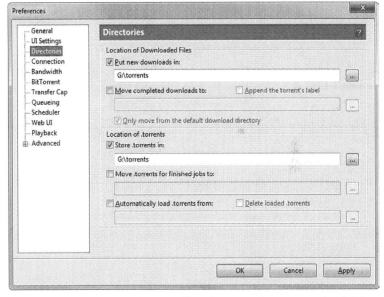

10   Turn on "Put new downloads in" and type or browse to the folder where you want content files to be downloaded.

BitTorrent shortens hard-drive life with continual read–write operations. If possible, don't download to the same drive or partition where Windows is located. Instead, use a dedicated internal or external drive or a high-capacity USB flash drive.

11 Turn on "Store .torrents in" and use the same location to store .torrent files that you specified in the preceding step.

12 For help with other settings, click the help icon 🅰 in the upper-right corner of the Preferences window.

13 When you're done, click OK.

To customize the µTorrent user interface (OS X):

1 In µTorrent, choose µTorrent > Preferences (Command+,) > Downloads.

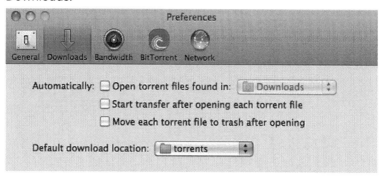

2 Turn off "Start transfer after opening each torrent file."

This setting prevents newly added torrents from starting auto-matically. After selecting which of the torrent's content files to download, you can start the torrent manually.

3 Click the "Default download location" drop-down list, choose Other, and then browse to the folder where you want content files to be downloaded.

BitTorrent shortens hard-drive life with continual read–write operations. If possible, don't download to the same drive or parti-tion where OS X is located. Instead, use a dedicated internal or external drive or a high-capacity USB flash drive.

4 Close the Preferences window.

Main Window

μTorrent's main window has three panes:

Category List.   This narrow pane (called the Sidebar in OS X) runs along the left edge of the main window and shows high-level torrent statistics, among other things. The information in this pane, which you can hide, generally isn't useful unless you manage scores of torrents or subscribe to RSS feeds.

Torrent Jobs List.   This pane runs along the top of the window and lists your current torrents with real-time statistics and status icons. It's the main part of the μTorrent interface and you can choose which information appears here.

Detailed Info Pane.   This pane, below the torrent jobs list, has tabs (General, Trackers, Files, Speed, and so on) that show detailed information about the torrent you select in the torrent jobs list.

To show or hide parts of the μTorrent window (Windows or OS X):

In μTorrent, choose the Show/Hide commands in the View menu to toggle visibility.

The View menu also shows the keyboard shortcuts for each command.

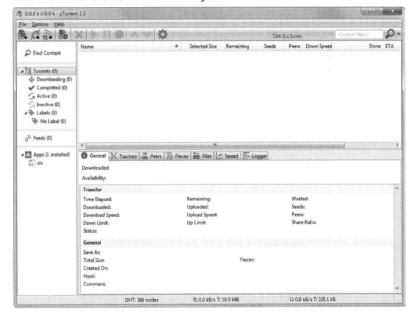

Torrent Jobs List

The torrent jobs list, where you'll spend most of your pirate time, shows at a glance the status of all your torrents. This pane contains a columnar list of torrents and their attributes indicated by column headings, which you can sort and customize in the same way that you would a file list in a folder window. The μTorrent help file describes all the available columns in detail (see "Getting Help" in Chapter 6). The most-useful ones are:

Name shows the name of the file or folder being downloaded. A color-coded status icon near the name indicates whether the torrent is down-loading (↓), seeding (↑), queued, stalled, stopped, or complete. (If you prefer words to icons, show the **Status** column.)

shows torrent's place in the download queue (1, 2, 3, . . .). When a torrent stops or finishes, the next queued torrent starts automatically. You can add any number of torrents to the list, but only a limited number of them will be actively downloading or seeding. μTorrent defaults to low limits to prevent bandwidth from being spread thinly over many torrents. To reorder torrents in the queue, see "Queueing a Torrent" in Chapter 10. To view or change queueing limits in Windows, choose Options > Preferences (Ctrl+P) > Queueing (in the left pane). In OS X, choose μTorrent > Preferences (Command+,) > BitTorrent.

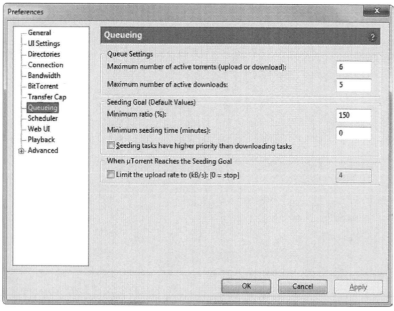

Preferences also lets you set seeding/upload goals (limits) for after torrents finish downloading. A torrent that's reached its goal has a blank in the # column; prior to that, it has an asterisk (*).

Selected Size shows the total size of the content files that you selected to download. (The less-useful **Size** column shows the total size of *all* the torrent's content files, regardless of whether you selected them.)

Remaining shows how much of the selected files is left to download. The related **Downloaded** column shows how much of the selected files has been downloaded so far. Selected Size = Remaining + Downloaded.

Seeds shows the number of seeders that you're connected to and, in parentheses, the estimated number of seeders in the swarm.

Peers shows the number of leechers that you're connected to and, in parentheses, the estimated number of leechers in the swarm. (Note that µTorrent uses *peer* to refer to what I and many BitTorrent websites call a leecher; for details, see Chapter 2).

Down Speed shows the current speed at which the selected files are downloading. If the torrent is very slow or seeding, its down speed is blank.

Done shows a graphical progress bar displaying the completed part of the download (0%–100%). Done = Downloaded ÷ Selected Size.

ETA shows the estimated time left (days, hours, minutes, and seconds) until the selected files finish downloading. If the torrent is seeding, its ETA is the time left until it reaches its seeding goal. If the torrent is stopped or has reached its seeding goal, its ETA is blank. A very slow torrent has an infinite (∞) ETA.

If you're using a private BitTorrent site that tracks your share ratio (see "Private Sites" in Chapter 7), you may want to show:

Up Speed shows the current speed at which the selected files are uploading. If the torrent is very slow, its up speed is blank.

Ratio shows the share ratio of uploaded data to downloaded data. (For initial seeders, this column shows the ratio of the uploaded data to the torrent's content size, starting from zero.)

To customize the torrent jobs list (Windows and OS X):

In the torrent jobs list, do any of the following:

- To choose which columns appear, right-click any column heading and choose a heading name to show or hide that column.

- To reorder columns, drag the column headings left or right.

- To resize a column, drag the right edge of its column heading left or right. To resize a column to fit its widest entry, double-click its heading's right edge.

- To sort the list, click the heading of the column to sort by. To reverse the sort order, click it again. Shading indicates the sort column. A small arrowhead near the column name points up (▲) for an ascending sort or down (▼) for a descending sort. To sort by multiple columns, sort by one column, hold down the Shift key, and then click the secondary column heading(s).

- To resize the pane, drag the horizontal separator up or down. (When you're over a separator, your pointer changes to a double-headed arrow.)

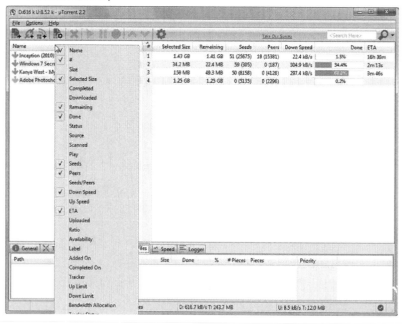

10

Downloading
Torrents

Now you're ready to hoist the Jolly Roger. The basic steps are below. Details follow.

To download a torrent:

1 Go to a BitTorrent website (Chapter 7 recommends a few).

2 Find a torrent.

3 (Optional) Read the torrent's description and user comments.

4 Download the .torrent file.

5 (Optional) Select the content files to download.

6 (Optional) Set the priorities of the selected files.

7 (Optional) Queue the torrent.

8 Start the torrent.

9 Wait until the download completes.

10 Remove the torrent.

Finding a Torrent

You can use Search, Browse, Recent, or RSS to find torrents (Chapter 8 has the details). Most sites index the same popular movie, TV, and music releases, but you may need to search a few sites for old or offbeat content. For help finding specific categories of torrents (movies, books, and so on), see the next few chapters.

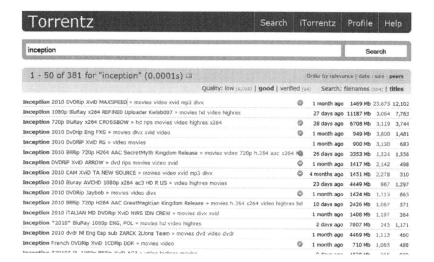

Reading a Torrent's Description and User Comments

You usually know what quality to expect from a popular, verified, or upvoted torrent, but if you have doubts or are downloading something less mainstream, click the torrent name and read the description and user comments on the torrent's main page. Initial seeders and release groups add torrent descriptions ranging from one-liners to elaborate technical details.

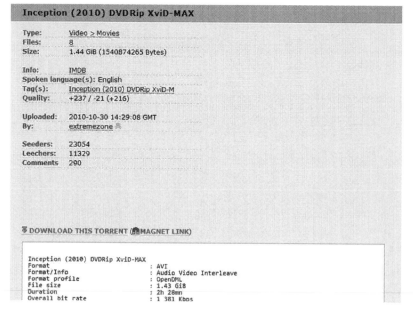

User comments can number in the hundreds. Among the "Seed!" and "Thanks!" shout-outs are quality ratings, software installation advice, questions or requests from peers, and warnings of fakes, malware, or nonstandard file formats.

Downloading a .torrent File

Most sites have **one-click downloads**, meaning a "Download torrent" link or icon (typically a down-pointing arrow) appears next to the name of each torrent in a Search or Browse results list. A download link also appears on the torrent's main page. Click the download link and, if given the option, open the .torrent file with μTorrent. Alternatively, you can save the .torrent file to your hard drive and double-click it to add it to μTorrent. Make sure that you download an actual .torrent file—some sites place other types of download links, including disguised ads, near the .torrent link.

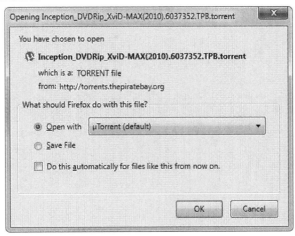

After a few seconds, the .torrent file opens in μTorrent. (Activate μTorrent yourself if it doesn't auto-open.) If you set up μTorrent as described in Chapter 9, the torrent will appear in the torrent jobs list but the content files won't start downloading.

Note: Recall from Chapter 2 that a .torrent file is a small text file that *points* to shared content files. Downloading the .torrent file is a separate, prerequisite step to downloading the content files themselves. When you installed μTorrent, it registered itself as the default program for the file type .torrent and the MIME type application/x-bittorrent. For details about file types, see Chapter 3.

Selecting Content Files to Download

μTorrent by default downloads every file in a torrent but that often wastes your time, space, and bandwidth (single-file torrents excepted). For media torrents such as movies, TV, music, photos, and books, it's easy to tell the tacked-on extras from the real files of interest. You don't need checksum (.sfv), executable (.exe), URL (.url), "Torrent downloaded from," and most text (.txt) files. You *may* want movie subtitles, music playlists, sample video snippets, cover art, screenshots, and NFO files. For media collections such as movie trilogies, TV series, or albums, you can deselect any undesired movies, episodes, or tracks.

Superfluous files in application and game torrents are harder to spot. In the simplest case, these torrents come with a single disk-image (.iso, .cue/.bin, or .dmg) or executable (.exe) file and an NFO file. But these torrents often carry many subfolders and files with unfamiliar extensions. In this case, download all files except obvious filler.

Some torrents include an **NFO** (.nfo) file containing release notes in text format. (NFOs are the pirate equivalent of Readme files.) For applications and games, the NFO file contains installation instructions and software requirements. For movies and music, the NFO file gives technical details such as the codec, bit rate, and resolution. An NFO's useful information, when present, is buried under the release group's ASCII art logo, credits, and other bits of self-promotion. In Windows, the default program for .nfo files is System Information (msinfo32.exe). To open an .nfo file in a text editor or reassociate the filename extension, see Chapter 3.

To select files to download:

1   In µTorrent, select a torrent in the torrent jobs list (the top pane).

2   In the detailed info pane (the bottom pane), click the Files tab.

The torrent's files are listed. You can customize and sort this list in the same way that you do the torrent jobs list (see "Torrent Jobs List" in Chapter 9).

3   Select the files that you *don't* want to download.

To select a file, click it or press the arrow keys until the file is selected. Or, in Windows, press the first letter of the file's name (repeatedly if necessary).

To select adjacent files, click the first file and then either Shift-click the last file or press Shift+arrow key. Or, starting from an empty area below the list, drag across files to select them.

To select nonadjacent files, Ctrl-click (Command-click) each file.

To select all files, press Ctrl+A (Command+A). To select *almost* all the files, select them all and then Ctrl-click (Command-click) the files that you want to deselect.

4   Right-click a selected file and choose Don't Download. (To undo this action, right-click a selected file and choose a priority.)

Excluded files are labeled "skip" in the Priority column.

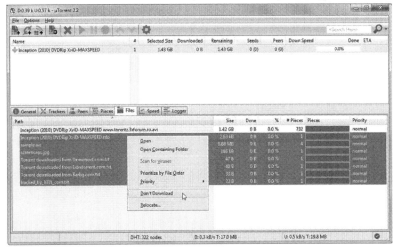

Setting File Priorities

µTorrent by default gives equal download priority to every selected file of a given torrent, but you can set any file's priority to change the speed at which it downloads. Files with higher priorities tend to download at faster rates than those with lower priorities. Priorities are handy for large media collections such as TV series, audio books, or music discographies; you can assign high priorities to the episodes, chapters, or tracks that you want to open first.

To set a torrent's file priorities:

1 In µTorrent, select a torrent in the torrent jobs list (the top pane).

2 In the detailed info pane (the bottom pane), click the Files tab.

   The torrent's files are listed. The Priority column shows each file's priority. You can customize and sort this list in the same way that you do the torrent jobs list (see "Torrent Jobs List" in Chapter 9).

3 Select the files whose priorities you want to change.

   Use the file-selection methods given in "Selecting Content Files to Download" earlier in this chapter.

4 Right-click a selected file and choose the desired priority (the default priority is Normal).

5 (Optional) Click the Priority column heading to sort the file list by priority.

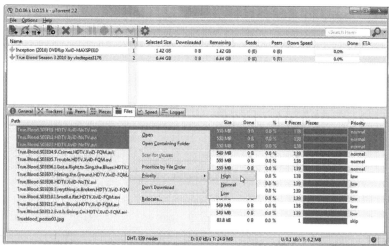

Queueing a Torrent

Recall from "Torrent Jobs List" in Chapter 9 that you can open any number of torrents but μTorrent will actively download only a small, fixed number of them at a time. A torrent's position in the queue, shown in the # column of the torrent jobs list, determines whether it's downloading. When a torrent completes downloading, the others move up the queue. You can reorder torrents to place more-important ones near the top of the queue.

To reorder torrents in the queue:

1   In μTorrent, click the # column heading in the torrent jobs list (the top pane) to sort the torrents by queue position (1, 2, 3, . . .).

2   Do any of the following:

- Right-click a torrent and choose Move Up Queue or Move Down Queue. In Windows, holding down the Shift key moves the selected torrent to the top or bottom of the queue.

- Select a torrent and press Ctrl+Alt+up arrow/down arrow (in OS X, press Ctrl+Option+up arrow/down arrow).

- (Windows only) Select a torrent and click the Move Up Queue or Move Down Queue button on the toolbar. Holding down the Shift key moves the selected torrent to the top or bottom of the queue.

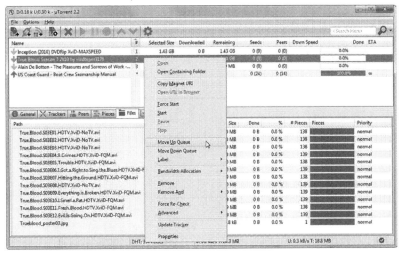

Starting a Torrent

To start a torrent, select it in the torrent jobs list and click the Start button ■ on the toolbar, or right-click the torrent and choose Start. If the torrent is near the top of the queue, the selected files start downloading to your hard drive in the folder that you specified (see "User Interface" in Chapter 9). If the number of active torrents has reached the maximum set in Preferences, the torrent is queued for later download.

Regardless of your queue maximum, don't start too many torrents at the same time or your download speed may suffer. I rarely have more than one or two actively downloading. Also, make sure that your upload speed is capped (see "Limiting Upload Rates" in Chapter 6).

Note: Right-clicking a torrent and choosing Force Start makes the torrent ignore the queue limit and start immediately. Forced torrents can't be stopped by seeding goals or the scheduler (see"Other Settings" in Chapter 6).

Waiting for the Download to Complete

Your download speed will be slow initially and then increase after a few minutes. µTorrent **scrapes** (requests) real-time statistics from the tracker, and displays them in the torrent jobs list and detailed info pane.

Name	#	Selected Size	Downloaded	Remaining	Seeds	Peers	Down Speed	Done	ETA
Inception (2010) DVDRip XviD-MAXSPEED	1	1.43 GB	1.22 GB	211 MB	76 (21142)	24 (9482)	466.1 kB/s		7m 53s
True Blood Season 3 2010 by vladtepes3176	2	6.44 GB	0 B	6.44 GB	0 (0)	0 (0)		0.0%	
Alain De Botton - The Pleasures and Sorrows of Work -...	3	360 MB	0 B	360 MB	0 (0)	0 (0)		0.0%	
US Coast Guard - Boat Crew Seamanship Manual		22.5 MB	0 B		0 (37)	0 (2)		100.0%	
The Odyssey		1014 kB	1014 kB		0 (32)	0 (3)		100.0%	

It may take minutes, hours, or days to finish the download depending on your connection speed, the size of the files, and the health of the swarm. The Done column shows how far torrents are from completion. Some things to do while you wait:

- Run µTorrent in the background and get on with the rest of your life.

- Change a torrent's file selection, file priorities, or queue position at any time.

- Shut down µTorrent if it's hogging bandwidth. When you restart, your torrents continue downloading from where they left off. Alternatively, you can stop a torrent without shutting down µTorrent.

To do so, select the torrent and click the Stop button ● on the toolbar, or right-click the torrent and choose Stop. In Windows, you can Pause ▮▮ a torrent if you need quick bandwidth. Unlike Stop, Pause doesn't drop your peer connections and is quicker to restart (though peers will drop *you* if you wait too long to restart).

- Open a complete file. You can open individual files as they finish downloading; no need to wait for the entire torrent to complete. To see which files are complete, select a torrent, click the Files tab in the detailed info pane, and then look at the % column. You can double-click any file that's at 100% to open it.

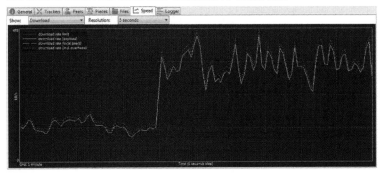

- Open the folder containing a torrent's contents. In Windows, right-click a torrent and choose Open Containing Folder. In OS X, right-click a torrent and choose Show in Finder (or select a torrent and press Command+R). If you set up µTorrent as described in Chapter 9, then double-clicking a torrent opens its folder.

- Track a torrent's download speed and other statistics. Select a torrent and click the Speed tab in the detailed info pane. Use the Show and Resolution menus to fine-tune the graph. The General tab also shows real-time and cumulative statistics.

Removing a Torrent

When a torrent is complete, the torrent jobs list shows 100% in the Done column and blank in the Down Speed column. (In Windows, you can show "torrent complete" pop-up messages by choosing Options > Preferences (Ctrl+P) > UI Settings (in the left pane) > "Show balloon notifications in tray.")

Recall from Chapter 2 that BitTorrent depends on peers continuing to seed after their torrents finish downloading. On public sites, you're not obligated to seed and there's no penalty for removing a torrent immediately after it completes (hit-and-run piracy). But if you want to be fair, continue seeding until your share ratio reaches one, meaning that the amount of data you've uploaded has equaled the amount of data you've downloaded. The Ratio column in the torrent jobs list shows your share ratio for each torrent (if this column isn't visible, right-click a column heading and choose Ratio).

When you're finished seeding, right-click the torrent and choose one of the following removal options:

Remove (or Remove From List) removes the torrent from µTorrent but leaves its .torrent file and content files intact on your hard drive. Use this option if you plan to reseed or send the .torrent file to someone.

Remove And Delete .torrent (or Remove Torrent File) removes the torrent from µTorrent and deletes its .torrent file, leaving the content files intact on your hard drive. The most common option.

Remove and Delete .torrent + Data (or Remove All Files) removes the torrent from µTorrent and deletes its .torrent file and content files from your hard drive, leaving nothing behind. Use this option if you're finished with the content files or discover that they're fakes or garbage.

Remove and Delete Data (or Remove Data Files) removes the torrent from µTorrent and deletes its content files, leaving its .torrent file intact on your hard drive. Rarely useful for completed torrents.

In Windows, you can change the default action of the Remove button on the toolbar: hold down the Shift key, right-click the button, and then choose a default removal option. To perform the default action, select a torrent and then click the Remove button or press the Delete key.

11

Movies and TV Shows

This chapter covers the naming conventions, file formats, and media players used for movie and TV torrents.

Movie Torrents

A movie torrent can have a name as simple as

> Casablanca

or

> King Kong (1933)

but most have names like

> Inception (2010) DVDRip XviD-MAXSPEED

The standard template for movie torrents is

> *title year source codec-group*

Title.   The movie's title usually appears as it does in IMDB (*imdb.com*) and can include a modifier like Director's Cut, Theatrical Release, Unrated, Extended, or, for series, Trilogy, Anthology, Collection, or Boxset.

Year.   The movie's release year helps when searching for remakes, new movies, and movies from a specific year. If you're looking for the 1951 version of the often-remade *A Christmas Carol*, include *1951* in your search phrase.

Source.   The source tells how the movie was copied and is crucial in deciding whether to download. See "Sources" later in this chapter.

Codec. A **codec** (short for coder/decoder or compressor/decompressor) is a small piece of software installed on your computer that lets you play back digital video that's been encoded in a certain way. Most movies use DivX, Xvid, x264, H.264, MPEG, or WMV codecs. Torrent releases now are so standardized and competitive that it's rare to find a movie that won't play on common media players.

Group. Organized piracy groups (called **scene groups**) race each other to become the first provider of quality movies. Each group appends its internet alias to its torrents' names. Certain groups appear repeatedly in the top movie torrents. One of the best known is aXXo, retired in 2009 yet whose legacy torrents are still going strong. If you download an older torrent, read the user comments to make sure it's not a fake with a forged group name.

Sources

Pirated movies are released with varying picture and sound quality over time. In general, early releases are worse than later ones because high-quality (digital) sources don't appear until the DVD goes on sale. When a better-sourced movie is released, inferior-sourced torrents start dying immediately. The common sources, from lowest quality to highest, are:

Cam copies are recorded in the theater by using a smuggled handheld or tripod-mounted camcorder. Audio is sourced from the camera's microphone. Quality is awful but offers the viewer a taste of being there: audience noises, people standing in front of the screen, ringtones, and bright little cellphone windows. Cams are released immediately after a movie previews or premiers.
Quality: Low.
Torrent labels: CAM, CAMRip.
Example: Faster 2010 CAM XVID LKRG.

Telesync copies look as bad as cams but sound better because audio is captured directly from the theater's sound system (possibly in cahoots with the projectionist). Telesyncs are released at the same time as cams.
Quality: Low.
Torrent labels: TS, TELESYNC.
Example: How.To.Train.Your.Dragon.2010.TS.XviD-PrisM.

Screeners are ripped (copied) from leaked review DVDs that movie studios send to critics, Academy voters, and film execs. Screeners show a movie's theatrical release but are degraded by sudden color changes, "Property of Whatever Pictures" overlays, or slightly fuzzy video. Screeners can appear at any time, even before cams.

Quality: Medium.

Torrent labels: SCR, SCREENER, DVDSCR, DVDSCREENER.

Example: The Social Network 2010 DVDSCR XViD WBZ.

R5s are ripped from Region 5 retail DVDs. (Region-coding prevents DVDs from working in players outside the countries where they're marketed—an irrelevance to pirates.) Region 5 includes Russia, Ukraine, North Korea, and other countries where legal but inferior DVDs compete with rampant piracy. R5s are released before DVD-Rips.

Quality: Medium.

Torrent label: R5.

Example: Knight and Day (2010) R5 XviD-MAXSPEED.

PPV-Rips are sourced from pay-per-view movies on hotel-room TVs. They're released before DVD-Rips.

Quality: Medium.

Torrent labels: PPVRip, PPV.

Example: Devil 2010 PPVRip IFLIX.

DVD-Rips are copied from retail DVDs and are the most popular type of movie torrents.

Quality: High.

Torrent label: DVDRip.

Example: The Graduate 1967 DVDrip XviD-Ekolb.

DVDRs are full copies of retail DVDs, including menus and bonus features but not copyright warnings, ads, and other cruft. Some DVDRs are compressed from their original dual-layer (DVD-9) format so they can be burned on cheaper, single-layer (DVD-5) DVDs. "Untouched" DVDRs are perfect copies of the original DVDs, cruft and all.

Quality: High.

Torrent labels: DVDR, DVD-R, DVD-Full, Full-Rip.

Example: Iron Man 2 (2010) DVD-R NTSC (eng-spa) [Sk].

HDTV-Rips are recorded from high-definition television signals, typically via a digital video recorder (DVR) or PC video-capture card. HDTV-Rips are labeled according to how they're sourced and encoded.

Quality: High.

Torrent labels: HDTV, PDTV, DSR, DVB, TVRip, STV, DTH.

Example: Tarzan.1999.720p.HDTV.x264.

BD-Rips and **BR-Rips** are copied from high-definition Blu-ray disks. BD-Rips are slightly better than BR-Rips. The resolution, 720p or 1080p, is the number of horizontal scan lines of display resolution. High-res files are big but yield sharp images. If you have a 720p display, don't bother downloading a 1080p file.

Quality: Very High.

Torrent labels: BDRip, BRRip, Bluray, MKV, BDR, BD5, BD9.

Example: Inception 720p BluRay x264 CROSSBOW.

Less-common (and low quality) sources include Workprint (WP), Telecine (TC), VHS-Rip (VHSRip), and Pre-DVD (PDVD).

TV Torrents

The standard template for TV torrents is

title episode source codec-group

For single-episode torrents, S*nn*E*mm* denotes the season or series and episode number. S02E11 means season 2, episode 11. Alternative formats include 02x11 and 211. The episode's title sometimes follows (or replaces) the episode number. Examples:

- Boardwalk Empire S01E12 HDTV XviD FEVER eztv

- Sherlock 1x03 The Great Game PDTV XviD FoV eztv

- The Simpsons S22E08 The Fight Before Christmas HDTV XviD LOL

- Family Guy - It's a Trap.DVDRip

- The.Biggest.Loser.S09E12.XviD-FattyMcGee

- Romanzo Criminale S02 E 9-10 ITALiAN HDTV XviD-SiD [IN] by ayubkhan

- The.Walking.Dead.S01E06.720p.HDTV.x264-IMMERSE

Multi-episode torrents labeled Season, Series, Complete, All, or Boxset contain all episodes from a single season or series, or every episode in the life of the program:

- True Blood Season 3 HDTV

- Sir Francis Drake Complete Series

- Looney Tunes [Golden Collection Boxset Vol 1]@Kidzcorner DVDRip

- Doctor Who Season 5 720p including Confidential 720p

- The Sopranos Seasons 1 6 Complete {gangafreak}

Daily soap operas, talk shows, and chat shows (whose torrents tend to die quickly) are labeled by air date (*yyyy-mm-dd*) or episode (S*nn*E*mm*):

- Jay Leno 2010 12 17 Owen Wilson HDTV XviD 2HD

- Oprah Winfrey 2010 11 23 Married A Killer Behind Bars HDTV

- Eastenders S26E191 WS PDTV XviD-W4F

- 11-17-2009 The Bold and the Beautiful mp4

Miniseries and documentaries are labeled sequentially as they air:

- BBC Ancient Worlds 2of6 The Age of Iron x264 AC3 HDTV MVGroup org

- The Great War and the Shaping of the 20th Century Episode Four

- National.Geographic.Great.Migrations.3of5.Race.to.Survive. PDTV XviD.MP3-MVGroup

- BBC - Leonardo da Vinci (complete 3 parts)

Sports are labeled by date, game, teams, event, or season:

- 2010 Vancouver Olympics Mens Snowboarding Halfpipe Finals HDTV XviD 2HD eztv

- NBA 2010 12 15 Lakers Vs Pacers HDTV XviD 433

- FIFA World Cup 2010 Group B Greece vs Argentina QCF

- NCAA Football 2010 10 02 Florida Vs Alabama HDTV XviD ESPN

- UEFA Europa League 2011 Group K Liverpool Vs FC Utrecht 720p HDT

- Beijing Olympics 2008 Opening Ceremony 720p HDTV x264 ORENJi

Shows are released as HDTV rips right after they air. Multi-episode torrents are released as HDTV, DVD, or Blu-ray rips after a season or series ends, or is released on retail disks. WS (widescreen) denotes a 16:9 width-to-height aspect ratio, rather than the older 4:3 ratio. For details about the codec and group, see "Movie Torrents" earlier in this chapter (one of the most prolific TV piracy groups is EZTV).

Video Formats

Most videos other than Blu-ray rips come as standard-definition **AVI** (.avi) files. The file size of a half-hour TV show is about 175 MB. A two-hour movie is about 700 MB (or twice that for higher-quality copies). At decent speeds, downloading an AVI file takes less time than watching it.

High-definition Blu-ray rips come as **MKV** (.mkv) or **MPEG** (.mp4, .mpg, .mpeg, .m4v) files. MKV also is called the **Matroska** format. Two-hour movies typically run between 2 GB and 12 GB, depending on content and quality (resolution, frame rate, audio streams, and so on). These files can take a day or two to download. If the torrent includes a sample video snippet, download and watch it first before committing to the entire torrent.

Less-common video formats include **QuickTime** (.mov), **Ogg** (.ogg, .ogm, .ogv), **Flash** (.flv, .swf), **RealMedia** (.rm, .rv), **Video Object** or **VOB** (.vob), and **Windows Media** (.wmv, .asf). VOB is a type of MPEG format. Adult video (porn) is the only genre that favors .wmv files. Some downloads come as disk images such as ISO (.iso) or CUE/BIN (.cue/.bin) files (for details, see "Mounting Disk Images" in Chapter 15). If you download a video in an unfamiliar format, search for the filename extension at Wikipedia (*en.wikipedia.org*) or *fileinfo.com*.

Peers who post user comments like

V:9

A:8

are rating, on a 1-to-10 scale, video and audio quality with respect to the file format: a "9" MKV looks a lot better than a "9" AVI. (Pirate film critics rate the movie itself by appending an M:7 or such.) Before you download, glance at the early comments for a ratings consensus and for mislabeling warnings (cams masquerading as telesyncs, or R5s as DVD rips).

Media Players

For Windows and OS X playback, use VLC media player (*videolan. org*); it's free and plays almost everything thrown at it. MPlayer (*mplayerhq.hu*) works well too. Avoid Windows Media Player and iTunes, which come with Windows and OS X but can't play many formats. See also Wikipedia's list of media players at *en.wikipedia.org/ wiki/Media_player_(application_software)*.

For iOS playback on iPad, iPhone, and iPod, try CineXPlayer (or VLC on jailbroken devices). For Android devices, there's VPlayer and

RockPlayerBase. These and similar players are available from Apple's App Store or Google's Android Market, or via Cydia for jailbreaks. Apps are updated to play catch-up to the number of supported video formats. Your best bet for smooth playback on mobile devices is a standard-definition AVI file using the DivX/Xvid codec.

For TV playback, I use Western Digital's WD TV Live. Similar players are made by ASUS, Iomega, LaCie, Popcorn Hour, and Seagate. Modern players let you play videos directly from a portable USB drive or stream them wirelessly from a networked computer. Older players, like Philips' DVP5960, are cheap but can't play many now-common formats. Avoid Apple TV. Out of the box, it's limited to iTunes-compatible videos (H.264/MPEG-4). If you already own one, poke around the web for jailbreaks and hacks to play unconverted AVI and MKV files.

AVI, MKV, MPEG, and many other video formats are **container formats**, meaning the filename extension alone doesn't dictate the video's encoding scheme. A given .avi file can use any of scores of available compression standards, hence the need for robust media players that can interpret a wide range of formats. Container formats are confusing and average users don't need to know much about them. A video either will or will not play and, if not, you can try a different player or download a different version of the same video. For technical details, start with Wikipedia's article about container formats at *en.wikipedia. org/wiki/Container_format_(digital)*.

Dubbing and Subtitles

In a **dubbed** video, the voices of the original actors are replaced by those of substitutes speaking a different language (specifically, the local language of a foreign market). A torrent's name, filenames, or release notes indicate the dubbing language:

- Spirited Away [Anime] [Eng Dub]

- Jet Li - Fist Of Legend [ENG DUB] (DivX)-AVI

- Toy.Story.3.FR.DUB.BRRip.720p.XviD-RalF

- Transporter 3 (Hindi Dubbed) DVDRip

Dubbing works well for animation, but for live actors ranges from distracting to comical (the canonical example being Godzilla movies where Japanese actors speak fractured, out-of-sync English). You're better off with an undubbed video that has **subtitles**: textual dialogue overlaid as captions at the bottom of the screen. Subtitles come in three flavors:

Hard subtitles, also called **hardsubs** or **open** subtitles, are merged in the original video and can't be turned off (think karaoke). Hardsubs are inflexible but require no special software or hardware for playback.

Prerendered subtitles, also called **closed** subtitles, are embedded in the video but can be turned on or off or display different languages (like the subtitles of DVD and Blu-ray disks). Newer formats like MKV can handle prerendered subtitles, but older formats like AVI can't.

Soft subtitles, also called **softsubs** or **closed** subtitles, come as separate files that you load in tandem with the video file. Softsubs are the most common type of torrent subtitles.

Support for closed subtitles varies by media player. In VLC media player, for example, you can use the Video > Subtitles Track menu to turn on or off subtitles, choose a language, or open a subtitle file.

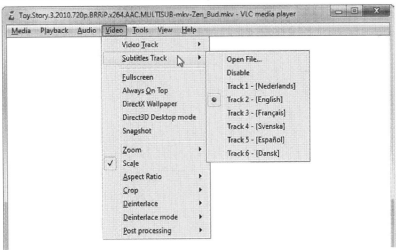

The most common and widely supported subtitle format is **SRT** or **SubRip** (.srt), named for the popular program that extracts video subtitles and timing cues from DVDs into text files. You can find a torrent's subtitle files in the same folder as the accompanying video or in their own folder named "Subtitles" or "Subs." Filenames indicate the language:

- Y Tu Mamá También - English.srt
- King Kong - French.srt
- EN.srt
- NL.srt
- Downfall (Der Untergang) [Eng][Subs].srt

To open subtitles at any time in VLC media player, choose Video > Subtitles Track > Open File. To load subtitles at the same time the video starts, choose Media (or File) > Advanced Open File, select a video file, turn on the "subtitles file" checkbox, and then select a subtitle file. Other options let you control the subtitles' font size and alignment.

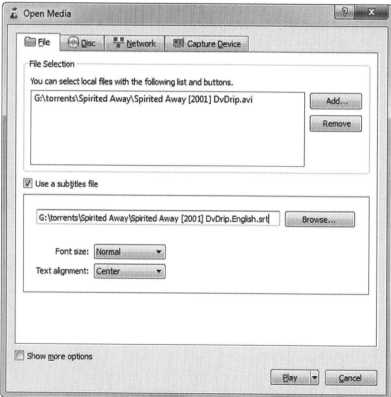

Other subtitle file formats include **SUB** or **SubViewer** (.sub) and **VobSub** (paired .sub and .idx files). For VobSub, open the .idx file, not the .sub file. Many other less-common formats exist. If you meet an unfamiliar one, read Wikipedia's article about subtitles at *en.wikipedia.org/wiki/Subtitles*.

Text-based subtitle files are easy to create and edit. (You can open an .srt file in a text editor to see its format.) If a torrent has no subtitle files, you can search for unofficial **fansubs** created by fans of movies and TV shows. To find fansubs, visit a subtitles site like *opensubtitles.org* or *subscene.com*, or search the web for what you're looking for followed by the word *subtitles* (for example, *battle royale subtitles*).

Other Videos

In addition to mainstream movie, TV, sports, and documentary torrents, you can find:

- Adult films (porn)

- Anime

- Awards shows

- Classroom videos

- Concerts and comedy shows

- Exercise and fitness videos

- Magic lessons

- Movie trailers

- Music videos

- Newsreels

- Interviews

- Radio program videos

- Short films

- Training courses, tutorials, seminars, and webinars

- War footage

12   Pictures

A sampling of vintage and modern pictures that you can download:

- Album, CD, and DVD covers
- Art and architecture (fine and otherwise)
- Blueprints, designs, and plans
- Cartoon, comic, and anime characters
- Celebrities, models, and naked people
- Family trips
- Games and athletes
- Graphics and icons
- Landscapes, seascapes, wildlife, and undersea life
- Maps, signs, and symbols
- Optical illusions
- Outer space
- Posters, ads, and logos
- Railways, planes, and vehicles
- Stock art and photos
- Tattoo designs
- Wars and crime scenes

Torrent payloads range from single pictures to large stock and museum collections, representing the work of artists, illustrators, graphic designers, photographers, photojournalists, drafters, architects, and cartographers. Image quality ranges from small, low-resolution photos to oversized, high-res desktop backgrounds (wallpaper).

Image Formats

The most common image formats are **JPEG** (.jpg, .jpe, .jpeg), **PNG** (.png), **TIFF** (.tif, .tiff), and **GIF** (.gif). **Bitmap** or **BMP** (.bmp) images are rare because, unlike the preceding formats, they're uncompressed and have large file sizes.

To view or organize image files in Windows, use Windows Photo Viewer or Windows Live Photo Gallery (the latter is a free download from Microsoft via Windows Update). In OS X, use Preview or iPhoto. Third-party image managers like Picasa (*picasa.com*) are available; read Wikipedia's list of image organizers at *en.wikipedia.org/wiki/Image_organizer*. The hardware players listed in "Media Players" in Chapter 11 can run slideshows on your TV.

Other formats include Adobe **Photoshop** (.psd) and **Illustrator** (.ai). An **Encapsulated PostScript** or **EPS** (.eps) file can be placed in professional design programs like those from Adobe and QuarkXPress. Some picture collections come as **PDF** (.pdf) documents (see "PDF Files" in Chapter 14).

If you download a picture in an unfamiliar format, search *fileinfo.com* for the filename extension or read Wikipedia's article about image file formats at *en.wikipedia.org/wiki/Image_file_formats*. To associate a particular image type with a specific program, see Chapter 3.

13 Music and Spoken Word

A sampling of audio files that you can download:

- Audio books, which can come as a single file, per-chapter files, or multiple equal-sized files that must be played gaplessly

- Classroom recordings, training courses, tutorials, and seminars

- Comedy shows

- Dance mixes

- Foreign-language instruction

- Historic speeches

- Literary and theatrical dramatizations

- Movie and musical soundtracks

- Music of every genre and venue from artists of every caliber, with downloads ranging from single pieces to discographies

- Podcasts and audio magazines

- Radio shows, news shows, and interviews

- Ringtones and computer system sounds

- Religious text readings

- Self-help and relaxation techniques

- Sound effects

Audio Formats

The most common audio format is **MP3** (.mp3). An MP3 file's **bitrate** largely determines its quality:

- The bitrate is between 32 kbps and 320 kbps (kilobits per second). Bitrates less than 128 kbps are low quality, akin to broadcast radio. 128–160 kbps is standard quality. 224–320 kbps is high quality, with 320 kbps sounding about the same as a CD.

- Better quality means larger files: the file size of a 3-minute MP3 is about 2.8 megabytes @ 128 kbps, 4.2 MB @ 192 kbps, and 7 MB @ 320 kbps.

- Expect diminishing returns: 128 kbps audio sounds hugely better than 64 kbps but only marginally worse than 256 kbps.

- For music, the torrent name, filenames, or release notes will sometimes give the bitrate; if not, you can view a file's bitrate in its Properties or Info window (see Chapter 3). Bitrates matter less for spoken-word audio, which are typically single-channel (mono) recordings with little dynamic range.

Other audio formats include **AAC** (.aac, .m4a, .m4b, .m4p, .m4r), **AIFF** (.aif), **FLAC** (.flac), **Musepack** or **MPC** (.mpc), **RealAudio** (.ra), **Vorbis** (.oga, .ogg), **WAV** (.wav), **WMA** (.wma), and many more. These formats may have better sound-quality/file-size tradeoffs than MP3, meaning they sound better at the same bitrate, but none has MP3's ubiquity. Every media player plays MP3s. Windows and OS X come with Windows Media Player and iTunes. Other popular media players include VLC media player (*videolan.org*) and Winamp (*winamp.com*). I prefer the simplicity of Media Player Classic (*mpc-hc.sourceforge.net*). See also Wikipedia's list of media players at *en.wikipedia.org/wiki/Media_player_(application_software)*. The hardware players listed in "Media Players" in Chapter 11 can play audio files on your TV. Some audio collections come with **playlists**, such as .m3u files, that you can open in your media player to play the accompanying audio files in a specific order.

If you download an audio file in an unfamiliar format, search *fileinfo.com* for the filename extension or read Wikipedia's article about audio file formats at *en.wikipedia.org/wiki/Audio_file_format*. To associate a particular audio type with a specific program, see Chapter 3.

14 Books, Documents, and Fonts

A sampling of books and documents that you can download:

- Academic textbooks and instructors' solutions manuals

- Comic books and anime

- Computer source code

- Course notes and reports

- Dictionaries, thesauri, references, and usage books

- Fiction and nonfiction of many periods, genres, and languages

- Foreign-language instruction

- Knitting patterns

- Magazines

- Maps, atlases, and travel guides

- Musical scores and songbooks

- Programming, computer, and technical books

- Religious texts

- Screenplays and scripts

- Tests and test-preparation guides

- Training courses, tutorials, and seminars

- WikiLeaks archives

PDF Files

The most common format for books is **Portable Document Format** or **PDF** (.pdf). PDF is a **fixed** page-layout format, meaning that you can't change a PDF file's font, text size, page size, page numbers, margins, columns, gutters, or whitespace. PDF works best for highly formatted documents like magazines, brochures, and screenplays, or typographically complex works like technical manuals, design specifications, math books, academic texts, and music, architecture, and art books.

PDFs are easy to read on large screens and tablets, but small-screened mobile devices show either an illegible miniature or a zoomed letterbox view of a partial page. Some ereaders reflow PDFs (badly).

For Windows, the most popular PDF viewer is Adobe Reader (*adobe. com/reader*). Depending on who you ask, Reader either works fine or is a buggy, bloated, chronically self-updating security hazard (PDFs can carry malware). Safer and svelter alternatives include Sumatra PDF (*blog.kowalczyk.info/software/sumatrapdf*) and FoxIt Reader (*foxitsoftware.com/pdf/reader*). See also Wikipedia's list of PDF software at *en.wikipedia.org/wiki/List_of_PDF_software*. If you download Adobe Reader, opt out of any accompanying crapware (such as McAfee Security Scan).

For OS X, use Apple's built-in Preview application or Adobe Reader. (In OS X 10.2 Jaguar and earlier, Preview doesn't support links in PDFs.)

For iOS on iPad, iPhone, and iPod, you can use Apple's free iBooks app to read PDFs. You also can attach the PDF to an email message and send it to yourself; to read the PDF, open the message and tap the attachment. Alternatively, transfer the PDF to your device and read it by using a third-party app such as GoodReader (my favorite), AirSharing, Documents To Go, or Aji Reader. All are available from Apple's App Store, or via Cydia for jailbreaks.

Amazon's Kindle DX and Kindle 2 and later have a built-in PDF viewer. Send PDFs directly to your Kindle via your @kindle.com address, or drag and drop PDFs from your computer to your Kindle via a USB connection.

Dedicated ereaders such as the Sony Reader and Barnes & Noble Nook have built-in PDF readers. Most smartphones have built-in PDF readers or third-party readers such as Documents To Go.

If you download a password-protected PDF that won't open or print, you can crack it easily with ElcomSoft's Advanced PDF Password Recovery (*elcomsoft.com*).

Ebook Formats

For novels and text-heavy works, avoid PDFs and look for books in **EPUB** (.epub), **Mobipocket** (.mobi), **Amazon Kindle** (.azw), **plain text** (.txt), or **HTML** (.html, .htm) format. Like webpages (and unlike PDF pages), ebook pages are screenfuls of text and graphics that **reflow** when you change the font or text size. EPUB is an open standard that all ereaders except Kindle support. Kindle supports .mobi and .azw. To convert among formats, use Calibre (*calibre-ebook.com*), an open-source, cross-platform library manager that's better than the shovelware that comes with some ereaders. See also Wikipedia's comparisons of ebook formats (*en.wikipedia.org/wiki/Comparison_of_e-book_formats*) and ebook readers (*en.wikipedia.org/wiki/Ebook_reader*). If you're looking for classics or works in the public domain, skip BitTorrent and browse Project Gutenberg's (*gutenberg.org*) huge library of free ebooks and audio books, which you can download in multiple formats.

Other Document Formats

A few other book and document formats:

- **Rich Text Format** or **RTF** (.rtf) is a common editable format that preserves most formatting, including fonts, styles (bold, italic, and underline), colors, text alignment, tab settings, and margins. You can open RTFs in just about any word processor. In Windows, the default RTF editor is WordPad. In OS X, it's TextEdit.

- Microsoft Office **Word** (.doc, .docx), **Excel** (.xls, .xlsx), and **PowerPoint** (.ppt, .pptx) are editable document, spreadsheet, and presentation (slideshow) formats. You can open them in Office or other office suites like Apple iWork, OpenOffice.org (*openoffice. org*), or LibreOffice (*libreoffice.org*). Microsoft also offers free converters and viewers for Office files at *office.microsoft.com/ en-us/downloads/office-online-file-converters-and-viewers-HA001044981.aspx*.

- **Compiled HTML Help** or **CHM** (.chm) is a fixed format that can include text, images, hyperlinks, and a linked index and table of contents. This format was originally intended for help files but now is common for ebooks. In Windows, the default CHM viewer is HTML Help Viewer. In OS X, use Chmox (*chmox.sourceforge.*

net) or iChm (*www.robinlu.com/blog/ichm*). In iOS, use iChm or ReadCHM, available from the App Store or Cydia.

- **DjVu** (.djvu, .djv), pronounced like "déjà vu," is a fixed format used for scanned books and documents. The DjVu website (*djvu.org*) lists free browser plug-ins and desktop viewers. I use WinDjView and MacDjView.

- **XML Paper Specification** or **XPS** (.xps) is a fixed-format PDF clone from Microsoft. To view XPS files, use Word, Microsoft XPS Viewer, Internet Explorer, or a Pagemark XPS Viewer browser plug-in (*pagemarktechnology.com*).

- Comic books usually come as PDFs, collections of numbered JPEG or PNG images (Chapter 12), or **Comic Book Archives** (.cbr, .cbz). To view archives in Windows or OS X, use Comical (*comical. sourceforge.net*). In iOS, many comic-book readers are available from the App Store or Cydia. The best-reviewed is Comic Zeal. Alternatively, you can extract an archive's separate image files by using one of the archivers listed in Chapter 5. Under the skin, comic book archives are actually RAR (.cbr) or ZIP (.cbz) files.

If you download a document file in an unfamiliar format, search *fileinfo.com* for the filename extension or read Wikipedia's article about document file formats at *en.wikipedia.org/wiki/Document_file_format*. To associate a particular document type with a specific program, see Chapter 5.

Fonts

Most fonts come as OpenType (.otf) or TrueType (.ttf) files. A surprising number of bad fonts are out there. The best ones are designed by professional typographers to look smooth onscreen and in print at any point size. OpenType fonts have extended character sets and advanced typography features used in high-end desktop publishing software. To avoid junky-looking knockoffs, get OpenType fonts from established foundries and professional type studios. See Wikipedia's list of type foundries at *en.wikipedia.org/wiki/Type_foundry*. To install a font file, double-click it or drag it to the Fonts system folder.

15 Applications and Games

A sampling of software that you can download:

- Business and home—accounting, communication, database, flowcharting, networking, personal finance, presentation, project management, reports and forms, schedule and contact management, spreadsheet, tax prep, training, travel, word processing

- Children—activities, art, early learning, games, interactive books, literature, math, nature, reading, reference, science, socialization, parental controls, problem solving, virtual pets

- Creative—3D, animation, clip art, cooking, fashion, hobbies, illustration, music and audio, photo and video editing, publishing

- Education and reference—arts, culture, dictionaries, encyclopedias, foreign languages, geography, history, literature, mapping, religion, science, script and screen writing, secondary education, sound libraries, test prep, typing, writing

- Games—all operating systems, mobile devices, and consoles

- Operating systems and servers

- Professional—3D modeling, architecture, drafting/CAD, forensics, IDEs and compilers, engineering, legal, mapping/GIS, mathematics, medical, statistics, virtualization, web development

- Utility—antimalware, archivers, backup, disk authoring, drive partitioning, file conversion, firewalls, image mounting, privacy, screen capture, security, text editors, voice recognition

Pirating software is dicier than pirating media (movies, music, and so on) because the former must be installed and poses a greater threat of malware (Chapter 4). When browsing for software torrents, look for popular releases by reputable piracy groups. Some installations are easy, but you're usually at the mercy of the torrent's installation instructions. These instructions come in a separate .txt, .nfo, .rtf, or .html file and range from lucidly comprehensive to cryptically terse. If you can't install or run a program, read the torrent's user comments to see whether someone else had (and solved) the same problem you're facing. You can also post your own questions, solutions, and experiences. Software piracy has its own vocabulary and techniques, described next.

Archives

For programs packaged as archives (.rar or .zip files), the first step of the installation instructions is "Extract" or one of its synonyms: expand, uncompress, unpack, unrar, or unzip. For details, see Chapter 5.

Disk Images

Often a program comes as a **disk image**, which is a single large file that reproduces the contents, structure, and behavior of an optical disk, hard drive, or other physical storage medium. If you've copied or backed up any music CD or movie DVD, then you're familiar with the idea. Think of a disk image as a digital copy of a program's original installation disk. Large programs can span multiple disk images.

The standard Windows disk-image formats are **ISO** (.iso) and **CUE/BIN** (paired .cue and .bin files). **IMG** (.img) files are equivalent to ISOs. Nonstandard images, which you should approach with caution, include **MagicISO** (.udf, .uif), **Media Descriptor** (paired .mdf and .mds files), and **PowerISO** (.daa).

The standard OS X disk-image format is **DMG** (.dmg). A less-common format is **CDR** (.cdr), an ISO-like format used by OS X's Disk Utility (you can change the filename extension from .cdr to .iso). Old OS 9 disk images have .smi or .img extensions.

If you download a disk-image file in an unfamiliar format, search *fileinfo.com* for the filename extension or read Wikipedia's article about disk images at *en.wikipedia.org/wiki/Disk_image*. To associate a particular disk-image type with a specific program, see Chapter 3.

Executables

An **executable** or **EXE file** is a program. (Technically, it's a sequence of instructions that performs specific tasks on a computer.) When you launch an application, you're actually opening its executable file. Windows application files have the extension .exe (notepad.exe, for example). OS X applications have the extension .app (iTunes.app). Small, standalone applications and utilities, which you can launch without installing, tend to come as executable files rather than as disk images.

Mounting Disk Images

Mounting a disk image makes it behave like a physical CD or DVD. A mounted image appears as a separate **virtual drive** in Windows Explorer or Finder windows, as though it were a real disk inserted into a normal CD/DVD drive. You can mount multiple disk images at the same time, from local or network drives.

Windows programs that can mount disk images include Daemon Tools Lite (*daemon-tools.cc*) and Virtual CloneDrive (*slysoft.com*). If you get Daemon Tools Lite, opt out of the bundled spyware (browser toolbar, Daemon search, and so on) during installation.

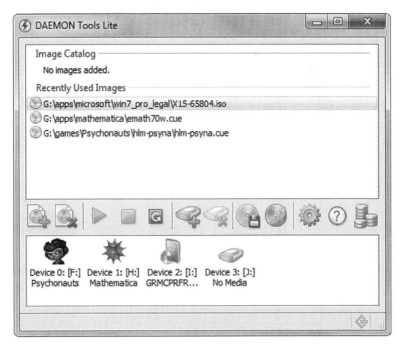

In OS X, .dmg files automount when you open them (you don't need a separate mounting program). To mount an ISO, use the built-in Disk Utility application (choose File > Open Disk Image) or the hdiutil command (in Terminal, type *hdiutil mount -help*).

File archivers (Chapter 5) can browse and extract the contents of ISOs and other disk images without mounting them.

See also Wikipedia's list of disk-image software at *en.wikipedia.org/wiki/Comparison_of_ISO_image_software.*

Burning Disks

Burning a disk records a disk image onto a writeable CD or DVD (to do this, your computer's optical drive must be able to write disks as well as read them). Installation instructions often have a "Mount or burn image" step, meaning that you can install a program by either mounting the disk image as a virtual drive or running a burned disk of the image. It's rarely necessary to burn a disk because image-mounting suffices in almost every case. Image-based software installations are faster than disk-based ones. You can install operating systems from images on bootable flash drives. You can bypass copy-protection requirements for physical disks by using disk mounters or software cracks. Console games are one of the few torrent categories where it's necessary or convenient to burn disks.

To burn a disk image in Windows, right-click an .iso or .img file and choose "Burn disc image." In OS X, use the built-in Disk Utility application (choose Images > Burn) or the hdiutil command (in Terminal, type *hdiutil burn -help*). For other disk-image formats, use a third-party disk-authoring program such as Alcohol 120% or PowerISO. See also Wikipedia's list of disk-image software at *en.wikipedia.org/wiki/Comparison_of_ISO_image_software.*

Keygens, Cracks, and Jailbreaks

Torrents for copy-protected applications and games include software countermeasures that bypass or remove the protection.

A **key generator**, or **keygen**, is a mini program that generates a product key or serial number that unlocks or activates software. Keygens are usually standalone executables, but some are command-line programs that you run in Command Prompt (Windows) or Terminal (OS X). If the keygen is an .exe file, then you must run it in Windows, even if it generates keys for OS X programs. (Don't be startled if a keygen plays a synthesized tune when you open it.) In some cases, a torrent will come with a typed list of keys instead of a key generator. You need a key when you install or first launch a copy-protected program.

A **crack** replaces or modifies software to disable a program's irritating DRM features (copy protection, expiration dates, trial limits, disk checks, ads, nag screens, and so on). Common cracks are .exe, .dll, .app, .plist, and other files that you copy to a program's installation or settings folders, overwriting the original (uncracked) files. Some cracks are standalone executables or registry (.reg) files that you need to run only once after you install a program. Overwriting or modifying original files or settings with cracks is called **patching**.

Installing a copy-protected program requires a keygen, crack, or both. The installation instructions should tell you how and when to apply them, and where they reside in the torrent or disk image (usually in a separate folder named "Crack," "Keygen," or labeled with the cracker's alias). The easiest programs to install are precracked (preactivated), requiring no special action by you beyond installation.

A **jailbreak** overrides vendor-imposed software lockdowns on a particular device. Jailbreaking an iOS device, for example, lets you bypass Apple's App Store and install cracked apps (.ipa files) on an iPad, iPhone, or iPod Touch via Cydia (*cydia.saurik.com*). Jailbreaking a video-game console lets you play pirated or homebrew games. Jailbreaks are common but they're not part of torrent downloads (they're a separate prior step). For more information, search the web for the name of your device followed by the word *jailbreak*. Related Wikipedia articles include "iOS jailbreaking," "Homebrew (video games)," and "Privilege escalation."

Installing Programs

Aside from generating keys and applying cracks, installing pirated programs is usually no different from installing legitimate ones. You must have administrator privileges on your computer to install software.

For Windows disk images, a program's install wizard should autostart when you mount the image or insert the burned disk. If it doesn't start, browse through the image or disk and open the program's setup file, usually named setup.exe or install.exe. Follow the wizard's onscreen instructions. Along the way, you may have to type or paste a key from the keygen.

Other types of Windows installers include Windows Installer (.msi) and executable (.exe) files. Some programs arrive unpacked in a hierarchy of folders and require no installation.

For OS X disk images, double-click the .dmg file or the icon of the burned disk, and then double-click the disk-image icon that appears on the desktop. Drag the program's icon to the Applications folder or to your home folder, or follow the instructions in the installer window.

In all cases, generate keys, apply cracks, and install and launch the program as the torrent instructs.

Index